Dedication and Endurance

Dedication and Endurance

ↄb

A True Story of Our Lives Before, During and After Dementia Alzheimer's

Conrad A. Stroh

Dedication

This book is dedicated to the memory of Elaine C. Stroh. She was the finest lady I have been blessed to know and love. Her life was an example of a never faltering love, free of judgement and disdain. Elaine was my trusted partner and she will always be my only love.

Acknowledgements

I WISH TO express my gratitude to Jennifer Hull for editing and providing the graphic artwork for my manuscript and to Linda Lou Hisaw for her proofreading efforts.

My profound thanks to everyone who provided the help and support necessary for me to tell my story. The support was rendered in various ways. Dr. Hettrick took the responsibility of Elaine as a patient long after she was diagnosed with Dementia Alzheimer's, guided us through a very trying time and advised us in an unbiased professional manner.

Family members were doing things on my behalf that I wasn't aware of. They included Tom and Bonnie Stevens, Jim Stroh, John Stroh, Craig Stroh, Mark and Lori Stroh. I also want to thank my grandchildren who took the time to visit Elaine. They are Jillian and Veto Nitti and their daughters Gia and Lilyana, Christopher Stroh and Anna and their daughter Rhiannon, Jessica Stroh, Jason Stroh and son Cameron, David, James and Michael Stroh.

Special thanks to friends and relatives including Elaine's lifelong friend, Elaine Freucht and daughter Kellie Vari, Cathy Stroh and Nancy Leva.

And finally, a heartfelt thanks to Jennifer McAlister with the Southeastern Wisconsin Alzheimer's Association and Tasha Orr-Holmes. These two women were my lifeline and I am forever in their debt.

Prologue

YOU MAY HAVE many questions about who is plagued with Alzheimer's disease, what happens while a person is afflicted and what you can expect after one succumbs to the illness. This book is an account of our family's encounter with an unexpected and devastating interruption in our lives. It is my sincere hope that our story will afford you the strength, perseverance and understanding to guide you through your journey.

Our whole experience was like a journey. It was the last one for my wife Elaine. Actually, it was also the last for me as Elaine's spouse. It truly was a journey because it was a constantly changing experience, like the scenery of a trip through the country side. Every day, a new challenge presented itself. Not necessarily bad, simply new. Along the way, as with any journey, detours were encountered and bypassed. The detours will be addressed throughout this book. Hopefully how we dealt with the unexpected will result in a better, less stressful path for you. It is my sincere wish that our story will provide a clearer road map to guide you on your journey and provide you with the will to continue.

I found the most important asset during these trying times was the incredible strength of our family. As in every case people go on with their daily routines and cope with unexpected situations. However, there are only a few of such instances that can remotely compare with the challenges presented with caring for a loved one with Dementia Alzheimer's. My inability to communicate with my Elaine was my biggest challenge. It was akin to caring for a baby and was accomplished by assumption and following my instincts. Unfortunately, there were many times when I incorrectly interpreted Elaine's signals and it resulted in great frustration.

It is imperative that the caregiver of an Alzheimer's patient takes complete advantage of all available help. However, your journey evolves, don't give up. Names and phone numbers of people and organizations that are willing and able to help are presented throughout this book.

Stay strong and God bless.

Table of Contents

Dedication··v

Acknowledgements··vii

Prologue··ix

Chapter 1   From the Beginning ··1

Chapter 2   Elaine's Turn ··9

Chapter 3   Looking for Answers ···19

Chapter 4   Drastic Changes···29

Chapter 5   A Lifesaver···39

Chapter 6   Security ···49

Chapter 7   "It's time."···57

Chapter 8   The Dreaded Day ··63

Chapter 9   A Different Environment ·······································69

Chapter 10   Rapid Decline···79

Chapter 11   The Inevitable···85

Chapter 12   Everything Changes ···89

Chapter 13   "Reflections"··99

Resources···111

About the Author···113

CHAPTER 1

⸙

From the Beginning

ELAINE AND I were both born in Chicago, IL. I entered this world in July, 1933 and she followed a year later in July of 1934. Initially we lived miles apart and it wasn't until our teen years when she moved into my school district and attended the same school as a neighbor girl. One day, I was at a friend's house and Elaine came to visit. That was it. I was infatuated. We were 16 and 15 at the time, and we saw each other at various functions. After some time, we became close friends and I eventually won her over.

Elaine didn't have a very pleasant childhood. Her mother died in 1940 and her father was drafted into the army and left Elaine in the care of her paternal grandparents. They didn't want her in their care and treated her badly. After her father returned home he remarried and she went to live with him and her stepmother. That was a terrible arrangement and when she was 15 she asked her maternal grandmother if she could stay with her. She was finally in a place where they welcomed and loved her dearly. When we first met she was still living with her father. I remember walking her home a few times just to be with her. She lived about 2 miles from her school.

My mid teen years moved at lightning speed. In June of 1951 I graduated from high school at 17. I turned 18 in July and my father died that August. Shortly after, my mother announced she was moving to California and said that I could go with her. I told her my girlfriend and my job were here in Chicago and that I wanted to stay. An aunt asked me to live with her I accepted the offer. I married from her house and Elaine married from her grandparents' home. By the way, I proposed to Elaine the day of my graduation.

During our engagement, someone told us that two can live as cheaply as one. We believed it and set the wedding date for September 20, 1952. The real reason Elaine and I married at such young ages was because we wanted a home of our own and a true sense of belonging.

Our first son, Tom, was born in October of 1953, and the youngest, Mark, was born in March of 1961. The others are James, John and Craig. After the five boys, Elaine gave up hope of having a daughter. Honestly, I don't believe I would have the patience to raise a daughter. With the boys, it was a well-defined expectation and not much latitude for failure. That didn't mean perfection; it just meant to give it your best effort. It seemed to work, because each of our sons has a strong work ethic.

Like most married couples, there were many situations which had to be confronted and resolved. Some were very serious, and tested our determination. One such incident was when, at age thirty, Elaine was diagnosed with Lupus. About a year after her diagnosis, I arranged for her to be evaluated at the Mayo Clinic in Rochester, MN. She made the trip alone, because no one was willing or able to stay with the boys. That was a devastating decision because of her weakened condition. The doctors at Mayo told her the Lupus was terminal. However, there was a possibility that, with complete bed rest for 2 years, the Lupus may go into remission. On her trip home, a gentleman sitting next to her on the plane thought she looked distressed and asked her if anything was wrong. She told him of her plight, and confided that she feared I would leave her when she gave me the news. She thought that a mother of five young children could no sooner stay in bed for two years than learn to walk on water. She told me the news when I met her at the airport. I told her not to worry; we would make it work.

We devised a plan of action by assigning specific chores to each of the boys. Tom took care of the laundry, Jim volunteered to do the ironing, John helped with the housework, Craig did the kitchen chores, which included washing dishes and Mark was assigned to bring lunch to Elaine. Preparing meals was the only remaining thing left to fulfill the family's needs. Elaine was familiar with the help people offered others in situations like ours. She told me that we would probably get some help with meals. However, she cautioned that the help may only last about two or three weeks. She was absolutely correct. It did stop and we were once again on our own. Fortunately, I knew how to cook. When I was nine years old my Mother worked and insisted a hot meal be ready when she arrived home each day. I was assigned the job. I disliked having to do that at the time, but it was a lifesaving ability that served us well. Knowing how to cook was also crucial to our survival when Elaine was stricken with Alzheimer's.

Our family plan worked, and after less than one year Elaine regained her strength, left the confines of the bed and the Lupus went into remission. We learned a valuable lesson during those trying times. When faced with a problem, the problem is yours and yours alone. How you face it will play a major role in how your life will transpire.

In July of 1967 we had saved enough for the down payment to purchase our first house. It was a wonderful time, and after several months, Elaine was strong enough to continue her task of caring for the family. Her greatest fear with her illness was that she would not survive to raise her boys. With the grace of God, she survived fifty-two more years. Over the years, our family grew to eleven grandchildren and six great grand-children. I believe the lesson learned is that "Winners Never Quit and Quitters Never Win." This is the mantra I try to impress on my sons, and my grandchildren

When I retired in 1997, we decided to sell our house in Illinois, and move to Wisconsin. While in Illinois, Elaine shopped and enjoyed lunch with her long time, and best friend every Wednesday. She approved the plan to move to Wisconsin with the promise she could continue her weekly shopping date. They met at Woodfield, in Schaumberg, Illinois. I agreed, and for more than seventeen years, the promise was kept. It wasn't at all inconvenient for me, because I also met a friend for lunch. He was a business owner, and therefore his time was flexible.

My preference for an area in Wisconsin was Kenosha. I had always wanted a boat and Kenosha's Southport Marina was exceptionally conve-nient. We purchased a new home in Kenosha, which was only two blocks from our son Tom. This arrangement worked out well. Tom's son was born two months after we moved in and Elaine was able to help care for our grandchildren.

I did purchase the boat and by doing so a lifetime dream was realized. The boat was docked in Milwaukee, Wisconsin and it had to be brought to Kenosha. We were still in the protection of the harbor when the broker said, "it's your boat, drive it." This monster I purchased was 38 feet long. The largest boat I had ever driven prior to this was a small ski boat. It was a windy day with waves 3 feet high in the harbor. Without any experi-ence boating on Lake Michigan, I didn't give any thought to what the conditions were when we exited the harbor. To my dismay I soon found the answer. We encountered following seas with waves 8 feet high. We did manage to make it to the Kenosha harbor, but only after the broker brought it in from Racine. I was absolutely drained of both physical and mental energy. Later, I hired a captain for one hour to teach me the principles of boat handling. I also read whatever I could find related to safe boating.

We enjoyed being on the water and took the boat out 52 times in the first year. People on the docks are very friendly and we became social with a few of them. One gentleman in particular became a very close friend and we met for breakfast at least once a week. Keeping the boat clean and in safe condition involved a considerable amount of time and energy. If you're not mechanical the cost to repair anything related to the boat may be very expensive. I'll give you one example. As I was showering the flexible tubing attached to the faucet broke loose. I located a dealer in Antioch, Il. who specialized in replacement parts for my type of boat. I explained my problem and after checking his catalog he found the part necessary to resolve the issue. He would have to order the part and the cost would be $286.00. I asked him not to order the part and I would contact him later. I went back to the boat and carefully scrutinized the faucet. I determined that the very small threaded connector (technically it's called a reducer nipple) at the top of the faucet was stripped. I stopped at a hardware store and bought the nipple for 26 cents. It was secured to the faucet and the flexible hose was affixed to it. Problem solved.

I served as a volunteer with the Coast Guard Auxiliary from 2000 to 2012. I joined a short time after I sold our boat. This gave me an opportunity to be active as a crew member on an Auxiliary facility and spend time on Lake Michigan. An Auxiliary facility is a privately-owned vessel sanctioned by the Government to assist the Coast Guard. The crew and boat are protected from liability. Technically the Government only reimburses the owner of the vessel for fuel. Those twelve years were very rewarding. Acquiring a crew rating on an Auxiliary facility was not a requirement for membership in the Auxiliary, but since I never served in the military, it seemed a good way to serve my country.

Conrad and Elaine, 9/20/1952

Our sons (L-R)
Craig, John, Mark, Tom, Jim

Dedication and Endurance

Conrad and Elaine, retirement, 1997

Elaine's 75th surprise birthday party

CHAPTER 2

— ❧ —

Elaine's Turn

LONG BEFORE ELAINE became ill with Alzheimer's, I had some serious cancer surgery. It was in January of 2002. During that ordeal Elaine was my savior. She took control of my recovery, along with the responsibilities of the household. I was 68 at the time, and I had really gotten out of shape. We joined a health club and I developed a workout regimen that would put me in compliance with the Coast Guard boat crew requirements. Through the spring and summer, I concentrated on being proficient as a crew member with the Coast Guard.

The Coast Guard Auxiliary traditionally sponsored a Christmas party for the Coast Guard personnel and their family members. The Auxiliary provided gifts for the children and door prizes for the Coasties (this was the accepted name for a Coast Guard member). Elaine also participated by assisting with meals and distributing gifts.

While at this particular party, a Coastie informed me that I only needed two "under-way" night operation hours to complete my certification requirements for my crew rating on the 41-foot boat. A minimum crew of three men was required and consisted of a Coxswain, Engineer and crewman.

We decided it was an ideal time to do this and we suited up with survival gear and got under-way. It was mid-December and very cold with zero visibility because of the total darkness. Lake Michigan wasn't very choppy, but the little sea spray we did encounter was enough to put a thin film of ice on the windshield and deck. Unfortunately, the defroster was inoperative. The engineer decided to go forward to clear the windshield. The only thing available to do the job was a credit card. The railings on the 41 were along the pilot house and atop the cabin with none along the sides of the deck. This was a dangerous situation for the engineer, after reaching the windshield, he was perched on the slanted roof of the cabin. I immediately went out to assist him. The only thing I could do was to grab him by the belt while I put my free arm around the cabin top railing for support. Everything worked out fine and my requirements for hours "under-way" were met. After passing the physical requirements, oral boards, and check ride, my crew certificate was issued. When I received my crew rating I was 69. I felt I could accomplish anything.

I went on patrol one Saturday at a time when Elaine was under a rigid medication schedule to combat an intestinal problem. I knew the patrol would probably continue until about 3:00 PM. As a precaution, I created a medication dosage schedule for her to follow. All the information was written on a white piece of paper with the appropriate pills placed on the page next to the corresponding time. When I came home, I was devastated to find that Elaine hadn't taken any pills. She was totally confused, and didn't understand what was written on the paper. I had explained everything to her before I left and she said that she understood when, in fact, she didn't have a clue what to do. A lesson learned the hard way. This revelation changed my whole course of action. As a result of that incident, I resigned from the Coast Guard Auxiliary, after twelve years of service. The sad thing about leaving was that Elaine had really enjoyed many of the social activities that included the spouses.

Dedication and Endurance

In the spring of 2010, we decided to update the house. It was purchased new in 1997 and required remodeling so that we could enjoy our later years in the house we loved. Elaine was seventy-six at that time and it all began with what was to be a modest budget. Our grandson offered to construct concrete counter tops. The only cost would be for the material. That sounded very inviting and we proceeded with the plan. Next, the cabinets were to be refinished and new hardware installed to minimize the cost. Shortly after all this inexpensive work was to begin, our grandson became very busy with his regular business and sadly informed us that he would not be in a position to provide the counter tops. Our initial inexpensive project turned into a massive remodel and when the job was finished, it looked like a different house. It also involved a large sum of money, and many hours of labor. And of course, you cannot complete a remodel project without new furniture and appliances. Oh well, just another miscalculated adventure. Actually, everything came together better than we had thought possible.

Around this time, Elaine began experiencing pain in her legs and back. She was under the care of a chiropractor and he recommended she have an MRI. The MRI disclosed some abnormalities which resulted in revision of treatments. While under the care of the Chiropractor, she experienced a fall as we were leaving a theater in Racine, WI. She tripped on the bottom step, fell forward and struck her head and knees on the concrete sidewalk. We took her to a local hospital where she was x-rayed, treated and released. When she asked me to complete the registration form, I didn't put any credence in her request, I simply attributed to the fact that she was upset.

Her treatments didn't seem to relieve her pain and I made arrangements for her to start physical therapy. It then became even more apparent that she was no longer able to complete a new patient form; she couldn't recall her address or phone number. After just two physical therapy treatments, her condition improved and she was in a much better state of mind. After the fall, she became completely dependent on me to complete all paperwork related to her medical needs.

About two months later a routine mammogram showed a tumor in her left breast. After a series of x-rays and a biopsy, the tumor was verified as being malignant. This was devastating news and, once again, I devised a plan of action. She was referred to a surgeon who immediately made arrangements to excise the tumor. Although the tumor was malignant, a mastectomy was avoided and only a small portion of the breast was removed. A few days after the surgery a decision was made to remove two lymph nodes from the affected area. This was done as a precautionary measure and proved to be beneficial. Sixteen radiation treatments were scheduled and left her with no sign of cancer. Score one for Elaine.

Over her lifetime, Elaine had spent a great deal of time reading. She had over 550 books in her library. Don't be impressed with the term library. The books were in dresser drawers, placed on the closet floors and stacked high on the closet shelves.

At the beginning of Elaine's dementia diagnosis, she was definitely aware of everyday activities. She had also enjoyed doing the puzzles where you have to circle a word that corresponds to a word from a list. There didn't seem to be any behavior or mental shortcomings that were noticeably disruptive. As time progressed her speaking abilities diminished. It was very frustrating, because she couldn't find the words to convey her thoughts. Trying to hold a conversation was like playing 20 questions. She would refer to objects as 'things,' because she couldn't recall the actual name of the item. This also presented a problem for her in the company of others. I ran interference for her, by partially answering an inquiry, with the hope she would pick up on the topic. After a while, everyone began noticing the problem, and I began avoiding putting her in embarrassing situations.

When you're very close to a situation, what is obvious to others may not be obvious to you. This was the case with me. Perhaps I was too busy or in a state of denial. There were times when it was difficult for me to put things in perspective. I know now that I was entering survival mode. We went on with our lives, and tried to make the best of unfamiliar circumstances.

Doctor visits were time consuming. Elaine's doctor's office was fifty miles from home and he was often late to his first office appointment. She liked this doctor and was his patient for 25 years when we lived in Illinois. She didn't want to see a new doctor and I respected her feelings. The visits were becoming more and more difficult because she couldn't find the words to convey her thoughts to him.

It reached a point when her doctor asked me to come into the exam room so there wouldn't be any misunderstandings when it came to medications. From that point on, I was placed in a position of often trying to determine what problem Elaine may have which needed attention. After controlling her medications and deciding which should be stopped or modified, a new responsibility emerged. I was now making serious decisions regarding Elaine's well-being.

When I brought up the issue of Elaine's declining mental condition the doctor didn't have anything to offer. He only suggested that she was having typical senior moments. Believe me, there is no such thing as a typical senior moment. There is nothing typical about losing your ability to communicate. He did prescribe a drug that was specific for dementia.

This visit with the doctor took place before Elaine had been diagnosed with Dementia Alzheimer's. After she was on this drug, I saw an advertisement that indicated the drug may possibly slow the effects of dementia. Not once did I hear of a drug capable of curing the disease. To my knowledge, there isn't any study that has established the rate of declination of dementia. However, the advertisements indicate that the drug **"may slow the progression of dementia."** How is it possible to slow something if you don't know how fast it's going? I had a discussion with her Doctor and stopped the medication. New medications have entered the market since Elaine's prognosis, all with the same caveat.

About a year after this incident, I noticed some decline in her cooking and baking skills. Although she couldn't even make coffee when we first married, she became a great cook and baker over the years. After all, what man in his right mind is looking for a good cook when he decides on his life partner? Our son Mark would jokingly tell his mother she was getting loopy. Little did he or anyone else in the family realize how serious her condition would become or the impact it would have. This would not only have a devastating effect on Elaine, but also on the rest of the family.

One day Elaine asked me to sit down. She wanted to talk to me. I knew she had something serious on her mind because she asked me to sit down. She then asked me to turn off the TV. When she asked me to turn off the TV, I knew it was definitely a serious matter. When I asked what she wanted to talk about, she very calmly said "You have a girlfriend don't you?" I started to laugh, and said, "Elaine, when do I have time for a girlfriend?" At the time, I didn't realize how serious she was. We were married over 60 years when this issue presented itself. Honestly, her thinking I had a girlfriend bothered me more than any other thing she could have said. Our marriage has always been built on absolute trust, and there was never any question about loyalty. Family members would tell me not to be upset, because she didn't understand what she was saying. Even though I understood she wasn't responsible for her actions, the implication hurt more than anything she ever did or said.

There were occasions when Elaine would get upset and say things that were hurtful. But shortly after she would cry and say how sorry she was. It was sad, because it was a genuine apology. I didn't know what to do, except to just hold her and tell her she had nothing to be sorry for and that I loved her.

These were the moments that tested my ability to change from being totally upset, to fully understanding that she had no control over her actions. I prayed for patience and understanding. Don't get the idea that I never felt like throwing in the towel. You cannot be expected to be a super human being. Once in a while it's only natural to vent your frustrations. That's what I kept telling myself, and at the time, I had to believe it or surrender. I learned very quickly that giving up was not an option.

It was about this time, that we decided to remodel the upstairs bathrooms. Elaine was having difficulty showering in a bath tub, and I decided a shower stall would be much easier and more convenient. The materials were purchased, and the renovation began. It took longer than expected because our son Craig had a mishap and wasn't able to work for about three weeks. Fortunately, we had a second bath, which sufficed in the interim. Elaine was delighted with her new shower. My son installed a granite bench and a hand-held shower, which made it very safe. Finally, we decided to remodel the guest bathroom, which was the final step to upgrading the house.

In early 2013 we were in the market for a new car. I had my heart set on a particular four door sedan, and was anxious to see if it was compatible with Elaine's mobility. The dealer was selected and we took it for a test drive. It was exactly what I had wanted. Elaine sat in the front seat and immediately said the car was difficult to enter and the seat was uncomfortable. I helped her out of the car and asked the salesman if there was a utility vehicle we could look at. He brought us one that seemed to perfectly suit our needs. Elaine had no difficulty getting in or out, and she was comfortable with the seats. We purchased the car and everyone was happy. Giving up the sedan was not an issue.

I asked Elaine if she would enjoy taking a trip to see our friends in Alabama. After visiting our friends for two days, we could continue on to Gatlinburg, Tennessee. She agreed and we proceeded with our plans. This trip to Gatlinburg would be one of several since 1971. Elaine loved being in the Smoky mountains, especially in the fall of the year. The colors are indescribably beautiful. Sadly, that was our last motor trip.

In May of 2013, I noticed Elaine was having some issues with her sight. After being evaluated by her Ophthalmologist, it was decided to remove cataracts from both eyes. She couldn't believe how much more pronounced the colors were, and her vision also improved. A few months after the surgery, the doctor performed a laser treatment to enhance her vision further. She had a peripheral test and had a difficult time ascertaining what she was expected to do. She did get through the test but it was very strenuous. It was the last time she was tested. Her ability to comprehend what was expected of her was no longer viable.

In 2014, Elaine began to have difficulty climbing the stairs. Her legs pained, and her balance was not good. There seemed to be a possibility she may fall and seriously injure herself. To prevent this from happening, a chair lift was installed to assist her to the second floor. This made the second floor readily accessible and allowed us to remain in the house and we avoided the dreaded chore of moving. I don't believe either of us could have survived the pressure of making the move.

She was more comfortable sleeping in the lounge chair downstairs, and only came up to shower and get dressed for the day. This arrangement was suitable, except if I heard a suspicious noise during the night, I would jump out of bed and run downstairs to see if she was alright. It's amazing how attuned one becomes when faced with the care of another. In the beginning, Elaine was able to operate the chair lift without any difficulty, or assistance. This afforded her the freedom to go upstairs at any time.

At about this time, I decided to construct a shed in the yard. This had been a goal of mine for several years. The perfect area was chosen, and my son Craig and I built the shed. It was exactly what I had hoped for, and it became a valuable asset. It provided ample room to store unused seasonal items, and kept the garage uncluttered. There was one caveat; I had to promise Elaine it would be my last project. Although a short time later, I did convince her that the garage would look better if it were insulated, dry walled and painted. It would be an inexpensive improvement and with the shed able to absorb the usual garage paraphernalia, the garage would be clean and uncluttered.

CHAPTER 3

Looking for Answers

As Elaine's disease progressed, her mental capabilities diminished. I spoke with a friend whose father was afflicted with dementia. She gave me some valuable information about the procedures available to determine the reason for the mental shortcomings. As per her suggestion, I called the Rush Medical Center in Chicago, and a Neurologist for an evaluation. We were anxious to determine what Elaine's problem was, and to start a program to control the effects.

Before the visit with the Neurologist, several tests were required. An order was issued and the testing was done at a local hospital, with the results forwarded to Rush. These tests included X-rays, a CAT scan, an EEG, and comprehensive blood work. After Rush received the results of the tests, we received a call to have Elaine evaluated. The test given at Rush was a cognitive evaluation.

The cognitive skills are rated from zero to thirty, with thirty being the best. Her score was twenty-one. She was also having difficulty with her verbal skills but that wasn't considered an issue affecting the outcome of the test. She was diagnosed with moderate Dementia Alzheimer's, and a re-evaluation in six months was suggested. She was reevaluated after seven months, and her cognitive skills score dropped from twenty-one to twenty.

After leaving Rush, I was perplexed. We were first told she had Dementia. Then we were told she had Moderate Dementia Alzheimer's. I was confused and didn't know if she had Dementia or Dementia Alzheimer's. My curiosity led me to the Alzheimer's Association web site at **alz.org**.

The web site states that dementia is not a specific disease. It's an overall term that describes a wide range of symptoms associated with a decline in memory or thinking skills severe enough to reduce a person's ability to perform everyday activities. Alzheimer's Disease is the most common type of dementia and accounts for 60 to 80 percent of the cases.

At the time of Elaine's evaluation, I had no idea that Alzheimer's was a type of dementia. There is no one test to determine if someone has dementia. Doctors diagnose Alzheimer's and other types of dementia based on careful medical history, a physical examination, laboratory tests, and the characteristic changes in thinking, day-to-day function and behavior associated with each type. To determine a specific type of dementia it would be necessary to see a specialist such as a Neurologist or Gero-psychologist. We were fortunate to have been recommended to the Neurologist at Rush.

When the doctor completed Elaine's reevaluation, she asked if I had gone to any support group meetings. I told her that I didn't need to, but she convinced me it would be beneficial.

I found a local support group through the Kenosha County ADRC (Aging & Disability Resource Center). They held their meetings on the third Monday of the month, at the Westosha Senior Community Center and I religiously attended every meeting. The Westosha Senior Community Center is located in Kenosha county, on highway "C", approximately 7 miles west of Interstate 94. The persons monitoring the meetings were very knowledgeable and experienced with the ramifications of Dementia Alzheimer's. The meetings were helpful by making me aware that many others were confronted with some of the same problems as Elaine and me. As a matter of fact, for about the first 4 months, I usually felt that most others had it much worse than me. At the beginning of my encounter with the support group, the effects of Alzheimer's had not manifested to a critical point.

The time spent at the meetings afforded me a couple of hours on my own. When I first started the meetings, Elaine was well enough to be left alone for a short time. After about 6 months I could no longer leave her alone and I asked my son Tom to stay with her while I attended the meetings. One of the participants mentioned that her husband attended a local Daybreak program. This was the first time I heard of Daybreak and I was interested in acquiring additional information. I received literature about the program and determined it would be advantageous for Elaine and me.

In February, 2015, Elaine began attending Daybreak and it was an absolute lifesaver for me. She attended three days per week from 9:30 AM to 3:30 PM. This allowed me time to do grocery shopping and other necessary chores. The Daybreak program is organized by KAFASI (Kenosha Area Family and Aging Services, In.) and can be contacted through the ADRC. KAFASI is also responsible for the Senior Dining program at the Westosha Senior Community Center. I began having lunch at the Senior Center and eliminated the inconvenience of preparing my lunch at home.

One of the most important things I became aware of at Daybreak was that they offered a "Virtual Dementia Tour." I highly recommend that anyone with a family member afflicted with dementia take the tour. The premise is to put you into the realm of what a dementia patient experiences. I won't go into detail, because it wouldn't be fair to you as a potential participant. I can tell you that the tour changed my perception of what my wife went through every day. Believe me, it changed my approach completely. Do this for yourself and your loved one. You will be a more effective caregiver.

While Elaine was at Daybreak, I had an opportunity to talk with a counselor at the ADRC. I was concerned about my ability to act as Elaine's primary caregiver and the responsibilities that entailed. I wanted to acquire information related to behavioral patterns of persons afflicted with Alzheimer's. The counselor told me that the progression of the disease is like a ball rolling down a slight decline. Without warning, the disease progresses as if the ball fell off a cliff. Then it returns to the progression of the slow decline, to another fast fall. When I asked what I may look forward to, she said, "it will only get worse." That bit of honest evaluation didn't help me at all.

Elaine's disease was increasingly diminishing her mental and physical abilities. It reached a point where I could no longer keep her at Daybreak. She stopped participating in activities and it became difficult for the staff to control her. The last few days at Daybreak Elaine was convinced I wasn't coming to pick her up and her anxiety level escalated. It was no longer advantageous for her, and definitely too upsetting.

Around that time, Rush Medical contacted me with an invitation to participate in a survey related to the effects of stress imposed on the caregiver of an Alzheimer's patient. The survey questions were conveyed electronically, as were the answers. The purpose of the survey was to gather data that may determine what level of physical or mental stress was imposed on the caregiver. The data could also be used to help guide a caregiver through the ordeal of coping with the unknown pitfalls that are almost certain to become part of daily life. The survey didn't consist of one series of questions. It involved several separate chapters, with questions related to each specific chapter. Several days passed between each chapter.

At the time, I participated in the survey, my stress level was low. I remember answering most questions with an answer that didn't indicate any mental or physical pressure. I may have been in a state of denial, or just too busy to realize how demanding my daily routine had become. If I had taken the survey nine months later, my account of the effects of being a caregiver would have been totally different.

When you are with a person plagued with Alzheimer's, there is no such thing as a typical day. I believe that is what makes it extremely difficult for a caregiver. You must be flexible, and have a very thick skin. As I mentioned earlier, it's very difficult to accept the fact that the person you're caring for and perhaps one that you undoubtedly love, doesn't realize how hurtful their words can be. There were very difficult moments.

I also had the misconception that being a caregiver was a routine job. Possibly because it was too early in the journey to consider our routine as being anything out of the ordinary. Family members would call and ask about Elaine. They also asked how I was and I didn't understand why they were concerned about me. It never occurred to me that there would be consequences for me caring for my wife. I discovered later that there are consequences. Without any apparent indication, your physical and mental health can be affected.

I did some research about a Living Will and Elaine and I decided to enter into a Living Will agreement. When she visited the emergency room her discharge papers included Living Will information. We decided to complete the required forms and had our neighbors witness our signatures.

As Elaine's condition worsened, I asked our attorney to check our various documents to verify that both Elaine's and mine were properly executed. This is extremely important. There are questions related to your desires for admittance to a nursing home or a short-term community-based residential facility. If you don't answer either "yes" or "no," your healthcare agent may only admit you for short-term stays for recuperative care, or respite care. Don't leave those questions blank. Be advised that a Living Will or Medical Power of Attorney is not valid without the signatures of two doctors on the "Incapacitation/Activation of Power of Attorney for Health Care" document. The key word here is "Activation."

My Power of Attorney for healthcare proved to be a life-saver. I had total control of everything related to Elaine's well-being. It allowed me to acquire medical records, discuss treatments with her doctor, and make decisions regarding her medication and care.

If you visit **Wisconsin.gov** or **your STATE.gov,** various legal forms are available for your convenience. I personally thought the Living Will forms received at the hospital were more comprehensive. There is also valuable information related to the **"Do-Not-Resuscitate" (DNR)** directive. Be advised that a DNR bracelet can be easily obtained and it clearly notifies others of your wishes. First responders to an accident or 911 call will not have access to your Living Will. If you don't have the DNR bracelet, the responders are required by law to do all they can to save your life. Important phone numbers and other personal information are also noted on the bracelet.

In October, 2014 I decided to have a whole-house generator installed. I couldn't take a chance of a power outage which could render the chair-lift useless. The idea of keeping a portable generator operating and having enough fuel for a prolonged outage didn't appeal to me any longer. Many things change with age and my ability and patience to properly maintain a portable generator, was at the top of the list. My greatest fear was the possibility of water seepage as a result of a heavy rainfall. Fortunately, we only experienced one power outage since the generator was installed. If we didn't have any outages, the peace of mind with the generator made it worth-while.

I became increasingly concerned that Elaine may not be getting proper nourishment. Our meals always seemed substantial and we certainly weren't lacking food, but I wanted to be sure Elaine's intake was sufficient. This is where I would like to caution you about scams. There are emotional episodes in our lives that may lead us to makes choices that are not in our best interests. Be very careful that products or services you purchase are approved medical protocol. Because of my concern for Elaine's nourishment, I was looking for a way to supplement our diet with healthful food.

As I watched TV one day I saw an infomercial on a food extractor. This was not a juicing machine. The machine pulverized fruits and vegetables, into a liquid form. The entire nutritional contents of the food were retained in the drink. A nutritionally balanced meal seemed like too much food for Elaine to consume. After extraction, the food will just fill a large glass with liquid nourishment. After researching the item, we purchased an extractor at a local store. The purchase included a recipe book which suggested the items to extract for each meal. Recipes were designed to offer the healthiest ingredients for each meal. This actually worked very well. Elaine was able to finish each meal and they were very delicious. I honestly couldn't tell you if they helped with her condition, but it did make meals easier for her to consume.

Elaine and I had always enjoyed going to the movies. Now she was plagued with a bladder problem, and had the urge to urinate almost every hour. This malady kept us from seeing the end of a few movies. She was able to shop with me for groceries and clothes. However, she would use the wash room before we left the house, and again when we arrived at our destination. This became a standard routine. The same scenario was true wherever we went.

One beautiful day and we decided to visit my sister in Elk Grove, Illinois. We were Southbound on I-294 when she suddenly announced that she had to use the washroom. I pulled off at IL 22 and drove east. I remembered that a gas station was fairly close to the interstate. As her discomfort escalated, the pressure to get her to a facility also escalated. I approached a red light, slowed, made sure it was clear and went through the light.

Further down the road I spotted a squad car and decided that if I passed him at a high rate of speed, he would turn on his lights and siren, and that would clear the way. He did, and I was able to approach the next light without anyone in front of me. The light was red. I slowed enough to make sure it was clear and went through a second red light. A gas station was at the corner across the intersection. I pulled into the gas station and the attendant quickly surmised the problem.

He ran toward us with the rest room key and the squad car pulled up directly behind me. I jumped out of the car and got Elaine into the rest room. I was so upset when the officer started to tell me of my many infractions, I simply told him to do whatever he had to do. I attended to Elaine and got her settled. The officer was very understanding. He realized I wasn't trying to pull a fast one and didn't charge me for going through two red lights, or not yielding to an emergency vehicle.

He said he had no idea how fast I was traveling when I flew past him. He gave me a speeding ticket that was for a lesser speed, so as to reduce the cost. I posted a $125.00 bond and was able to take a safe driving test electronically. Passing the test expunged the ticket. The fine and cost of the test totaled $240.00. We abandoned our plan to visit my sister and we went home and tried to enjoy the rest of the day. One of the many things I learned at this time was not to dwell on interruptions to routine. It doesn't change a thing and you can go on as if nothing happened. Easy to do? Absolutely not. Try it anyway, you may be surprised.

I told my son Tom about the incident and said I would do the same thing if it happened again. He informed me of the unnecessary chance I took with the possibility of causing injury or death. He strongly suggested I rethink my actions. He was absolutely correct. It only proves that children, even when they are 62, can have more sense than the parent. SOMETIMES.

CHAPTER 4

— ⚭ —

Drastic Changes

AT THIS STAGE of Elaine's illness, she was becoming more and more forgetful. We would go to the grocery store and as usual, I would drop her off at the door and park the car. I asked her to wait just inside the entry. This arrangement worked fine, until one day she went to the ladies' room, and got confused when she finished. When I entered the store, and didn't see her standing near the entry and I assumed she had gone to the ladies' room. I waited, and after some time, I went to the door and called out to her. There was no response. I panicked. I felt like a parent who had a child wander off in a store. After frantically looking, I found her standing at the end of an aisle. She had no idea anything was out of the ordinary. I simply took her by the hand and we continued shopping. Another lesson learned.

Although I could no longer leave her alone in the store, she could still accompany me while we shopped, and sometimes Elaine could wait in the car for a short time while I shopped. This worked just fine, until one day when I stopped for fuel. As I was leaving the station store, Elaine was trying to exit the car. She had no idea where she was going; she simply wanted to leave the car. This change in behavior presented a new problem. I could no longer leave her alone under any circumstances. This also marked the end of her shopping and luncheon dates. There were occasions when her friend's daughter offered to shop with the ladies and I would drive Elaine to her friend's house and find something to occupy my time for a couple of hours. Although this only happened twice, it proved to be a nice break for both of us.

When Elaine could still be alone a short while, I met with a Coast Guard Auxiliary associate for breakfast at least once a week. I also enjoyed breakfast with a former boat dock mate. He was also retired and our conversations were always interesting. These minor respites gave me an outlet and afforded me the opportunity to converse with someone other than Elaine. These breakfast meetings were my only remaining contact with the Auxiliary and it was an enjoyable way of hearing all the news about my former colleagues. I looked forward to these breakfasts. Unfortunately, they also came to an end.

As time progressed, everything that was once a normal part of Elaine's life was quickly becoming unfamiliar. She could no longer dial a telephone. If she wanted to call someone, I would dial the number. When she finished with a call, she didn't know how to hang up the phone. These were the moments that required a great deal of flexibility and understanding on my part. My top priority when we were faced with this type of situation was to ask God to please give me the patience and understanding to help Elaine maintain some degree of comfort. I knew my only hope was to ask for guidance from a higher power.

As the disease progressed simple chores became impossible for her to accomplish. I had been told that it was best to keep the person afflicted with Alzheimer's busy with familiar tasks. I would place the dishes, napkins and flatware on the table, and ask her to set the places for dinner. This only worked for a short time. I simplified the task by asking her to just get the napkins. This also became difficult for her to understand.

Finally, I asked her to separate the flatware. Even though I placed the flatware on the island directly above the proper drawer, she stood there for about 20 minutes, trying to separate the flatware. When she finished, the forks were with the spoons, the knives were with the forks, and so on. It was heart wrenching to see her struggle with such a simple task. I encouraged her and complimented her for doing a good job. Eventually I simply stopped asking her to help with even small tasks.

One day, I noticed that my cash, which was wrapped around my ID cards and the car fob, were all missing. It was futile to ask Elaine what she did with them, so I started a search of the house. After some time, I successfully found the money, car fob, credit cards and ID cards scattered on the bed in the guest bedroom. Elaine had a good supply of cash that I had given her over the years. The cache was made possible by her ingenious method of paying for her purchases. I would routinely give her money for birthdays and Christmas with the idea that she was best qualified to choose her own clothes. I know it was an easy way for me to avoid the chore of shopping, but it did save a lot of time by not having to return unwanted items. When she shopped she paid with a credit card and I would receive the bill at the end of the month. That way she cleverly avoided spending her cash and I didn't mind at all.

She and her best friend would occasionally spend a week at a summer home in Michigan and having her own money gave her a sense of independence. I placed her money in an envelope and kept it in my desk drawer. She knew where it was and I assured her that it was available at any time. I looked in the drawer one day and found the envelope with the money was missing. When I asked where she put it, she just looked at me and didn't have a clue where it was. The hunt was on. My first thought was that she threw the money in the garbage. We continued to search and the money was eventually found under some clothing in a dresser drawer. This whole routine happened a second time and, again, I assumed she threw it away.

Elaine continued having difficulty recalling words and it was difficult to have a sensible conversation. She knew what she wanted to say but couldn't find the proper words to express her thoughts. This was very frustrating for her and me.

She was plagued with an unexplainable pain in her upper chest or head. The first time it happened, I was convinced she was dying. As a matter of fact, I called my son Mark and told him of my concern. Looking back, it was strange that I didn't call 911. I can only reason that, when this happened, I panicked. I believe that was the first time in my life I wasn't able to think rationally.

On April 4, 2015 Elaine had one of what I will refer to as an "incident." She was having severe pain in her upper chest and head. We went to the local hospital where they tested for heart and brain abnormalities. She was released when the hospital could determine no obvious cause for the pain. Throughout the summer of 2015 she had several incidents of upper shoulder and head pain. Her mobility was diminished and she started physical therapy treatments. I convinced her that she would be more comfortable if she slept in bed rather than the lounge chair. She agreed, and the new arrangement made it much easier for me to care for her.

After several more incidents, I decided to take her to the hospital where her doctor was affiliated. It was fifty miles away, but I felt she would be more comfortable with her doctor. The date was June 12, 2015. She was admitted and, after running the same tests performed at our local hospital, it was found that she had pneumonia. I went home for the night, and returned early the next morning. When I walked into her room, I joyfully said, "good morning!" She responded with, "you bastard!". I was stunned. She was convinced that her room was in the basement of the hospital. I imagined that because her testing was performed in the basement and she thought her room was down there also. To my surprise, her doctor was not available, and she was attended by one of his associates. I asked where her doctor was and didn't get a reasonable response. That didn't help the situation or contribute anything to make her more at ease.

The pain continued periodically, and my concern increased. On August 28, 2015, I contacted Mayo Clinic for an appointment. They had records of her being treated for lupus in 1963. When I explained her symptoms, I was transferred to the cardiac center, and an appointment was scheduled for October 20, 2015. Elaine was angry with me for making arrangements at the Mayo Clinic. After I explained the situation in greater detail, she calmed down and soon forgot about the whole thing.

Rather than wait another month for the Mayo Clinic appointment, I decided to take Elaine to a renowned hospital in Milwaukee, WI. The reputation of this hospital is close to that of the Mayo Clinic. It seemed logical to acquire treatment closer to home. On August 31, 2015, I took her to the emergency room. We arrived at 12:30 PM. Chest X-rays, and a CAT Scan were performed, and she was placed on a monitor.

The tests were evaluated, and the doctor informed us that there were no indications of any abnormalities. Just as the doctor was explaining the results of the tests, Elaine had another incident and her blood pressure reached 210/94. I looked at the monitor and read the stats. The elevated blood pressure reading may have been an anomaly. I had no formal medical training and was certainly not qualified to criticize the doctor's judgement.

However, after witnessing her reaction with the pain and elevated blood pressure reading, I was surprised the doctor simply decided her blood pressure medication needed adjustment and suggested we follow up with a visit to her family doctor. We arrived home at 8:00 PM. I prepared a light meal for us, and made Elaine as comfortable as possible. It seemed futile to pursue the issue any further. Although the pains never did subside, they became more bearable.

After the last hospital visit, and prior to her appointment with the new doctor, I continued to monitor Elaine's blood pressure and kept a log of the results. For the next month, she experienced both good and bad days. She awoke one morning after a good night. Her spirits were up and I got her showered, dressed, and prepared a nice breakfast. I was advised that her pain medications be increased, from 2 to 4 per day. The day went well until about 9:45 when she had another episode.

The next day she was fine and survived the day without any major events. Sunday arrived, and she felt well enough to attend church services. We went to a restaurant for an enjoyable breakfast, and visited our son John afterward.

Two days later, Elaine was not doing well. She refused to take her medications. It just seems to be a waiting game at this juncture. I thought it best to wait, administer her medications later and see what would happen. Taking her to the ER was no longer an option. She endured going to three different hospitals for the same condition, and none of them offered any sensible conclusion. As I mentioned before, she was simply advised to see her family doctor.

When her doctor failed to see her during her former hospital stay, I decide it was time to acquire a new doctor. Our son Tom's physician was conveniently located and he spoke highly of him. I asked Tom if he objected to having his doctor see Elaine. He didn't so I called Dr. Brian Hettrick in Paddock Lake, WI. Unfortunately, he couldn't see her until October 19, 2015.

We were grateful he accepted Elaine as a patient. He was great and only seven miles from home. The necessary paper work was completed and we proceeded with the introduction of her new doctor. Thankfully, Elaine liked him and was very comfortable with him. He performed a comprehensive exam, drew blood, and reviewed her medications and medical history.

He is a no-nonsense doctor and didn't waste any time. He mentioned that he had been treating Alzheimer's patient for ten years and was familiar with the consequences of the disease. His disclosure enforced our confidence that we made the correct decision. He decided to test Elaine's cognitive ability. She scored a 10 out of 30. This indicated a drop of 10 points since her last test at Rush Medical Center. That was not good.

A short time after Elaine's visit with Doctor Hettrick, she once again started with the accusations of me having a girlfriend. If you recall, she did this for the first time about two years prior and I laughed at the idea. Now she was obsessed with the thought. Her ranting bordered on vile hatred and continued off and on for two days. She insisted that no one was supporting her and we were trying to get rid of her. When she did settle down, she cried and apologized. Once again, I told her she had nothing to be sorry for. I held her in my arms and assured her that I loved her and would always be there for her. This was another time when it was difficult to dismiss the feelings of hurt.

I kept a log for a short time and this is an entry I made on November 11, 2015. *Today started out badly, without any improvement at all. At one*

point, we just sat and reflected on our lives together. I began to doubt she
will ever feel better.

The next day she was feeling good. This was a big improvement from the last three days. We went for a drive, and purchased new reading glasses for Elaine. The next day was Sunday, and she awoke feeling weak with pain in her legs. I helped her to the bathroom, and we went downstairs for her to relax in the lounge chair. After a while, I convinced her to clean up and dress, because Craig and John were to stop over that afternoon.

Later that month, we were invited to Tom and Bonnie's for Thanksgiving dinner. We cancelled that morning, because Elaine didn't feel well enough to go. Tom and Bonnie were kind enough to bring dinner to us. Mark heard of our plight, and brought a broccoli casserole. The food was delicious, and we made the best of what could have been a disappointing situation. That evening I innocently glanced at my watch and Elaine said I should leave soon if I wanted to be with my girlfriend.

The church we had been attending was located a long distance from the parking area and the congregation area was several steps from ground level. I registered at a new parish with the entrance at ground level, and the parking area was next to the entry. This configuration was less strenuous for Elaine. The church was located about twenty minutes from our house. She accused me of choosing a church that far from home because I was ashamed of her, and because my girlfriend belonged to the parish.

She couldn't get past the distrust. If she had reason to believe I was unfaithful, I would understand. However, our marriage was based on absolute trust, and neither of us ever gave the other a reason to doubt that trust. On December 4, 2015 my journal entry read, "Elaine is asking for a divorce. She is convinced I have a girlfriend. It is now 9:00 PM and she shut all the lights, TV, and lay down on the sofa. Her dislike for me is evident, and she will not converse with me at all. She has been this way for the last two days, and shows no sign of letting up. I don't know if I should pursue putting her into a facility."

The next day Elaine was in a terrible mood. She refused to have breakfast, and I had trouble administering her medications when she wouldn't eat. Tom said he would stop over, and I invited him to have breakfast with us. Tom eventually persuaded her to eat breakfast and take her medications.

Her terrible mood continued in its fourth day. In my log, I wrote: *The down times seem to last longer. I'm trying to decide what would be best as an alternative to keeping Elaine at home. She is so convinced that I'm cheating, she continuously dwells on it. I don't know what to do.* The frustration of not having an answer to the problem was beginning to wear me down. Somehow, I had to find relief for myself and Elaine.

Later that day, I was working in my office and became aware of unusual sounds. It was Elaine, struggling up the stairs with a large framed picture. This was a gift from John that included a picture of us taken on our wedding day flanked by three separate verses. One was dedicated to his feelings for Elaine, another to me and a third referencing us together. It was beautifully done and was hung in a prominent location in our home. When I asked where she was taking the picture, she told me she was going to break the glass and remove the picture of us. I asked her to let me do that for her. She agreed and I put the remaining picture in the shed for safe keeping.

The next day she came into my office and her obsession with me having a girlfriend had now progressed. She accused me of having children with another woman. Later that day, I found her taking any pictures she found of us together and cutting me out of them.

I was beginning to think there may be something more bothering her besides the Alzheimer's. I began fearing that she may try to hurt me and I gave serious consideration to have her evaluated by a psychiatrist. I didn't know of any other option. Her behavior was so confusing and not having any training in recognizing the effects of Alzheimer's, I simply decided to wait and continue to take it one day at a time. This was a classic example of when a caregiver should seek professional help.

CHAPTER 5

—— ❧ ——

A Lifesaver

It was early December, 2015. Elaine was in a bad mood and I was desperate for information that may help me contend with her escalating problem. My prayers were answered. I remembered conversations with the ADRC informing me that the Alzheimer's Association had a hot line available 24 hours a day.

It was a mild day with just a slight chill in the air. I couldn't call with Elaine present, so I went out to the shed to call the **Alzheimer's Hotline, (800-272-3900).** As the call was going through Elaine came into the shed. She was so upset, she was shaking and out of control. In a screaming voice, she proceeded to swear and accuse me of calling my girlfriend. I was dumbfounded. I just stood there with the phone in my hand not knowing if I should start talking or simply hang up. Elaine needed immediate attention so I stopped the call, got her into the house and tried to calm her down.

After some time, she did settle down. Her hatred for and distrust of me had escalated to a boiling point. I even considered that it may be best if we separated. Without me around, her tension might be relieved. I was thinking about the old adage, "out of sight, out of mind." Later that day, she informed me that she wanted to change her name. The constant uncertainty of her actions led me to doubt if there was any hope that I could continue to care for her.

One night I was awakened at 1:30 AM by the noise of Elaine trying to open the front door. I stopped her from leaving and we sat while I reminded her of all the good times we shared. She listened, and after a while, she calmed down. We returned to bed at about 3:00 AM. She woke me at 6:00 AM wanting breakfast. When we dressed and came downstairs, she said she wasn't hungry and didn't want anything to eat.

I went ahead and prepared enough eggs, toast and tea for both of us and she completely finished her portion. She took her medication and we were off to another day. I learned another lesson. Alzheimer's Disease clouds the victim's memories and there are times when they don't remember from one moment to the next. This proved to be true many times in the future.

Craig stopped by later that morning to stay with Elaine while I shopped for groceries. While at the store, I found the answer I was looking for. I called the Alzheimer's Hotline and spoke with Jennifer. She became my lifesaver. I explained that it was me that called the day before and apologized for hanging up. She said, "I'm so glad you called. I heard what was going on and I felt so sorry for you." After explaining what had transpired she informed me that when a person afflicted with Alzheimer's reacts with such radical behavior, **it may be a result of an underlying problem.** I emphasized this statement to make you aware of how significant this could be. She suggested that I take Elaine to the doctor as soon as possible. I called the doctor's office and an appointment was scheduled for December 10.

Later that day she continued to act as though she despised me. Once again, she accused me of having a child with another woman. Nothing seems to help her understand the fallacy of her suspicions. I was continually being confronted with behavior completely out of the norm and I was getting desperate for help. When I completed the Rush Caregiver Survey, one of the questions was, "Do you feel trapped?" At the time my answer was "no." If asked that question now, my answer would be a resounding, "YES!" How much has changed in such a short time.

The day before the December 10 doctor visit, things seemed somewhat normal. I said "somewhat," because I wasn't sure what "normal" meant anymore. Although she agreed to see the doctor the following day, everything changed when I told her that had I arranged a meeting with the Alzheimer's Association at 11:00 AM the same day. She became very angry and again began accusing me of having girlfriends and even that I had fathered children with several women. I couldn't even imagine the mental turmoil she was obviously enduring. She also told me she didn't want to live, wanted to change her name and wouldn't cooperate with improving her health. That last statement scared me. It put me on alert and it was definitely a topic of discussion at the meeting with the doctor that morning.

Nothing I said to Elaine seemed to help her. I thought she might refuse to see the doctor the next day, so I called Jennifer from the Alzheimer's Association and told her of Elaine's behavior. She suggested we meet on a date shortly after the visit with the doctor and a new date was set. She also asked that I bring someone with me. A second person may provide additional information or remember something that I might not register with me. Mark's wife Lori accompanied me to the meeting.

Later that evening we had a long talk and Elaine became very calm. We enjoyed reminiscing about our many motor trips and cruises. We had driven through all of the lower 48 states, flew to Hawaii and cruised to Alaska. One trip in particular came to mind. Elaine had always wanted to see Banff, Canada. She suggested that we fly to San Francisco, rent a car, drive to Banff and return the car to Seattle. She didn't want me to drive the entire trip since I had driven on so any trips in the past. She thought if we flew most of the way I could relax and get more enjoyment out of the trip. I agreed and told her it was a great idea. We didn't realize the distance from San Francisco to Seattle by way of Banff was going to be a 3,000-mile trip. However, we did avoid a 4,000-mile drive. I was so relieved after our conversation and had my best night's sleep in over a month. Living with an Alzheimer's patient was like riding a roller coaster. The only difference was that when riding a roller coaster you at least had an idea when the dramatic ups and downs were coming.

Finally, it was the day of Elaine's scheduled appointment with Doctor Hettrick. She woke me at 1:00 AM and demanded I quit faking sleep. She said she heard me close the front door, which I had not. After convincing her to get back in bed and relax, I fell asleep. At 4:15 AM she tuned on the light and told me to get up. She was losing the concept of time and that last interruption ended my sleep for the night. While I was helping her get dressed, I reminded her of the doctor's appointment and she informed me that she would not go to the doctor. I didn't dwell on the matter and hoped she would forget about it. I learned that you cannot reason with an afflicted person and the best way to cope was to simply ignore the issue or change the subject.

So far it hadn't been an easy morning. It was only 9:30 AM and she was constantly talking about my suspected girlfriend and other children. If you recall, in the beginning it was just a girlfriend: then it was a girl-friend and a child. The scenario then escalated to several girlfriends and finally it concluded with my having several children.

After a while she did settle down enough for me to get her to the doctor. She wouldn't allow me to assist her from the house into the car. As we drove, her demeanor was unsettling. She started to rant and become very agitated. When we arrived at the doctor's office, she didn't want any assistance getting out of the car or any help into the office area. Fortunately, there weren't any stairs to climb. She despised me and didn't care who knew it. She wouldn't sit next to me or allow me to help her with her coat.

Even after living with the situation for a long time, it was sad to see her in that condition. I never did become immune to her accusations. I accompanied her into an exam room and the Physician's Assistant came in. Elaine immediately went into a devastating rant about me. I excused myself and left the room. The doctor got an earful for almost twenty minutes. She explained that Elaine was extremely upset and she suspected Elaine was suffering from a urinary tract infection (UTI). This suspicion was confirmed with a simple urinalysis.

A fast acting medication was prescribed and we picked it up on the way home. When we arrived home I immediately administered the medication for the infection. An anxiety drug was also prescribed to help alleviate Elaine's stress. After administering the medications, I took her to the second floor and tucked her in bed. She was obviously totally exhausted. Except for the bathroom breaks she slept through the night. I felt so sorry for her; she had been going a mile a minute for two days.

The initial dose of the anxiety drug was pretty strong. I wasn't familiar with the effects of the drug and I became concerned when she became unsteady as she walked. After reading drug information, I became alarmed. It specifically mentioned that the drug could cause imbalance. I feared that I may be giving her an overdose. I immediately called the doctor's office and expressed my concern and I was assured the amount given to her was acceptable. This new medication became a way of controlling her emotional upheavals. Eventually she was placed on a schedule of one pill in the morning and one in the evening. They were very small which made it easy for her to ingest.

Early in her diagnosis, Elaine could shower independently. Her balance problems increased with the new anxiety medication, and it was apparent she was no longer capable of showering herself. From that day on, I showered her. My routine had been to take my own shower before going to bed and didn't have a need to shower with her in the morning. It would have been difficult for her to remain patient while I showered. From that day forward our morning routine was pretty well established. Upon awakening, I would ask her to stay in bed for a few minutes while I shaved, brushed my teeth, washed and combed my hair. That may seem like quite a lot to do, but it only took about five minutes.

Many mornings she wouldn't wait. She would go into her bathroom and I could hear the water running. With that, I stopped what I was doing to check to see if she was alright. There were times when she had started to wash her face, not realizing she was to shower in just a few minutes. She couldn't be left alone and she didn't understand why I asked her to wait for me.

Under normal circumstances, if she waited for me I would escort her into her bathroom, help her brush her teeth and shave a small amount of facial hair from her chin. After rinsing the soap from her chin, I placed a hot wash cloth on her face. She absolutely loved that. As a matter of fact, she loved it so much she would moan in delight. She was very conscious of an unobtrusive bit of hair on her chin. I purchased an electrolysis device I saw advertised on TV. This helped, but didn't entirely remove the hair and definitely did not eliminate her obsession with the problem. I showered her every day and washed her hair every other day. One day while in the shower, I jokingly mentioned how exciting this shower would have been 65 years ago. She got the message and we both laughed.

After showering, I proceeded to help her dress. She chose her own clothes for the day, but she needed help dressing. Helping her get dressed made me proficient at guiding a woman in putting on a bra. However, I don't actually believe that talent is much in demand.

As time went on, Elaine became more easily confused and her mobility had diminished considerably. She also regularly lost her appetite. Thankfully we had the food extractor and she was able to get proper nourishment with the liquid drinks. After a day or two she would be back to eating regular meals. The anxiety pills were all that was keeping her manageable.

Managing daily surprises became my new normal. Any unfamiliar noise would put me on alert, and many times it was fortunate that I was present to prevent a disaster. One example was when it became apparent Elaine was no longer able to safely operate the microwave oven. One time she set the microwave for 12 minutes and 30 seconds when the time was to be set for 1 minute and 23 seconds. She was heating up a cup of coffee and it seemed to be taking a long time. I checked and when I saw the time, I stopped the oven. She couldn't be trusted to operate it. The plug should have been disconnected to make it inoperable. I didn't think of doing that and, luckily, she never tried to heat up anything again.

Another incident was when she went upstairs and a short time later I heard a loud noise. I ran up to see if she was alright and found that she was rearranging a plastic plant and it fell to the floor. She would often spend long periods doing nothing constructive and on occasion something destructive. I found earrings that she had ruined by bending them out of shape. But hiding her jewelry was out of the question. Spending time by simply moving it from one place to another, or wearing various pieces seemed to give her a lot pleasure and it kept her occupied.

Bed time often meant a continuation of the day's difficulties. It just got dark and the issues remained. She was still plagued by having to use the bathroom almost every hour. Her movements while getting out of bed would wake me and I had a hard time getting a good night's sleep. Eventually I would become accustomed to her new routines and could manage to sleep and somehow be alert if there was a problem in the bathroom. Perhaps it was a sixth sense or I was never in a sound sleep in the first place.

Elaine was becoming more and more difficult to control. I remember one day when she awoke in a bad mood and I gave her an anxiety pill after our morning ritual. By all appearances it was going to be a difficult day. We finished breakfast and I suggested we take a ride to get some fresh air and a change of scenery. She agreed. We could be out on county roads just five minutes from our house and wouldn't be bothered with urban traffic.

All went well for about twenty minutes until she began a rant about my girlfriend. My only option was to turn around and go home. Luckily the medication began to take effect and she calmed down. Many times after one of her verbal attacks, she would cry and say "I'm sorry" over and over again. She was still somewhat lucid and didn't understand why she felt so terrible. I explained about her condition and she said she had no idea it would be that bad. She also indicated that she had no desire to continue on like that. I heard these words in the past and my concern elevated whenever she expressed that thought. The rest of the day was uneventful. She slept in the lounge chair and I went into my office and checked my computer. It was about 11:00 PM when we finally went to bed.

One morning after her shower, Elaine began crying. She said that she didn't feel well and that there wasn't any fight left in her. I had planned to stop at the bank that morning and hoped she would feel well enough to join me. She slipped into a vile mood and I called Tom's wife, Bonnie to stay with Elaine while I went to the bank. Shortly after I arrived home, Bonnie left. Elaine went into the kitchen and began destroying utensils. I convinced her to stop the destruction in the kitchen. I left her alone while I sat in the family room.

Just as I thought everything was fine and Elaine was keeping herself harmlessly occupied with something of interest, I heard a loud bang, jumped up and found her trying to tear the seat cushion and foot rest from the chair lift. This was new behavior and I realized that she had to be monitored more closely. I felt the only way to maintain her morale was to increase the dosage of her anxiety medication and I began administering one pill every six hours.

CHAPTER 6

Security

I NEEDED A plan. I couldn't physically restrain Elaine and decided it would be best to try to interest her in something she had enjoyed in the past. Lori had given her a beautiful coloring book with several colored pencils. Elaine was able to draw very well and the idea of setting her up with the coloring book seemed like it would be a great outlet for her. That didn't work. She tried, but couldn't comprehend the principle of coloring within the lines or what colors to choose. She actually started to scribble at the bottom of the pages with a crayon. I almost cried. It was becoming clear that her condition would never improve and, undoubtedly, would continue to deteriorate.

It was mid-December 2015 when Elaine began trying to leave the house. She would put on her coat, grab her purse and open the door. I could hear her open the door and would ask where she was going She would simply say, "I have to get out of here." The issue of Alzheimer's patients leaving the house was mentioned several times at the support group meetings. Now with the problem very close to home, I knew something must be done to contain her and protect her from harm.

When locked, our storm door was very difficult to unlock. The locking device required several turns and doing that was more than she could comprehend. The patio doors were secured by placing a piece of PVC plastic tubing in the lower track between the doors. This was also beyond her cognitive ability. The only problem was when she unlocked the patio door and tried to force it open. She had the strength to shake the door so violently I thought she would destroy it. After failing to open the patio door she eventually gave up trying.

The basement door was secured by installing a new door knob with a key lock. I cut the key to the width of the door casing and placed it above the door where it was completely out of sight. The only remaining egress was the garage. She didn't remember how to turn the locking button on the door knob. However, I couldn't take a chance that she may accidently figure it out. To be safe, the garage door opener was disconnected. The remote opener was the only way to open the doors and I kept it in a place where it could be retrieved quickly if necessary. The most important thing was to keep every means of egress hidden from Elaine.

Her condition was digressing rapidly and I was literally sleeping with one eye open in the event she needed help in the night. She continued to have bladder control problems and awoke frequently to use the bathroom. The second time she fell at night when going to the bathroom I sprang out of bed to check on her and was relieved to find she had fallen on the carpeted floor and was not injured.

Elaine was becoming increasingly more destructive and demanding. If you are a caregiver and find yourself in a situation similar to mine, you may wish to seek professional advice to create a safe environment for your loved one. This task is very difficult and may seem endless in that situations constantly change that require some modification to your most recent plan. Whatever happens, don't be discouraged. You *will* prevail. You *must* prevail. Your survival and the survival of your loved one depends on it.

Dedication and Endurance

At one point, Elaine was no longer able to operate the chair lift. It simply required the user to press an "up" or "down" button at the end of the armrest. The device came with a remote control and, when necessary, I was able to operate it for her. One night, she refused to sit in the chair and I couldn't force her. I went up to bed and before I fell asleep I heard heavy breathing and strange sounds. I jumped out of bed and found her crawling up the stairs. With some effort, I was able to assist her to the second floor and into bed.

Now another problem presented itself. I had to devise a way to prevent her from leaving the second floor. If she fell down the stairs the result could be disastrous. The chair lift had a feature that allowed the user to swing the chair ninety degrees. This allowed the user to step off the chair into the hallway and not on the stairs. I noticed that if the chair was swiveled away from the hallway, it was difficult, if not impossible to get past it. From that moment on I was able to sleep more comfortably by simply turning the chair ninety degrees. That solution didn't present itself soon enough.

Earlier in this book, I emphasized the importance of caregivers not becoming discouraged and prevailing in their endeavor. I also mentioned the necessity of constant modifications to caregivers' plans as new situations arose. This happened once again. One night I found Elaine trying to force her way past the chair at the top of the stairs while it was turned away from the hallway. This required her to step off the hallway floor and balance herself on the top step while trying to squeeze past the chair. I was awakened by the sound of her struggling to get past the chair. If she made it past the chair, I'm convinced she would have fallen down the stairs. Now, what to do? My only option was to confine her to the bedroom.

My first idea was to close the bedroom door at night. At first, she didn't realize that she could have reached the stairs by simply opening the door and walking to the end of the hall. However, after a few days she found that opening the door would set her free. Now my only recourse was to sleep on the floor next to the chair lift. She didn't understand why I was sleeping on the floor and she asked me to come to bed.

After doing this for a few days I decided to ask Craig to stay for a while so that I may be able to get some sleep in my bed. He slept in the bedroom nearest the chair lift and was able to monitor Elaine's movements. With Craig there, Elaine stayed in the room but her constant activity kept me awake most of the night. I didn't want to inconvenience Craig and told him we would be alright if he left. After he left I continued to close the bedroom door and Elaine may have thought that Craig was still in the house because she succumbed to the confinement of our bedroom at night.

As Elaine's condition worsened, I decided to speak to an attorney about property distribution, powers of attorney and wills. The attorney was recommended by my insurance broker and tax accountant. When I asked for a recommendation, without hesitation, they each named Gene Brookhouse. That was the best recommendation I could expect. I made an appointment and we went to see him.

After reviewing our circumstances, he suggested we register our property with a **TOD, "Transfer on Death"** deed. This meant that upon our death the ownership of our house would transfer to the named beneficiary without going through probate. He also executed the durable power of attorney and medical power of attorney. Fortunately, Elaine was still able to sign the paperwork. Soon after, her signature evolved to nothing more than a wiggly vertical line.

We also completed a form called an "**Authorization for Final Disposition Instructions.**" This final act may not seem important, but if you are not able to depend on a family member or close friend, you may not have your final wishes respected. These forms are all available through your State Department of Health Services.

Early in February, 2016, Elaine suffered another UTI. She had an accident in the bathroom at home and another about 1:30 AM. I took her to the doctor. He prescribed medication and gave us a recommendation for a Urologist. The frequency of the UTIs was a concern and the Urologist did a bladder scope to rule out any serious problems. The results didn't indicate any bladder problems, nor did they provide any reason for the reoccurring UTIs. Elaine really wasn't aware of what was happening and I went on caring for her as best as I could.

In March of 2016, Elaine was scheduled for physical therapy to help her maintain her balance while walking. Her imbalance may have been as a result of the effects of the anxiety drug. This appointment was made two weeks prior and I cancelled at the last minute because she wasn't feeling well. We had cancelled several times in the past and I was ready to give up. After the last cancellation, she never had any more physical therapy sessions.

Mark was celebrating his birthday and asked us to join him, Lori and a few close friends for pizza. When he asked what our topping preference was, I suggested he order anything except pepperoni. I explained that it was Elaine's least favorite. Elaine liked Mark and Lori's friends and while we waited for the pizza the conversation was very enjoyable.

The pizza was brought to the table and amongst them was one with pepperoni. I couldn't believe it when Elaine ate nothing but the pepperoni pizza. This was another example of how the disease controls the mind and fails to differentiate the victim's common likes and dislikes. If you recall I mentioned how she had "no" to breakfast and, just in the short time it took to scramble the eggs, she changed her mind. This happened quite often and you may want to make a note of that behavior pattern.

The night of March 24, 2016 was one of the worst of my life. Elaine wandered around all night. I had spent two days arranging her clothes closet and by morning she was wearing several blouses and her clothes were strewn all over the floor. She was belligerent and unmanageable with all the symptoms of another UTI. I took her to the doctor in the morning and he verified my suspicions and prescribed a new medication. The UTI put her in a vile mood and I left the exam room while she proceeded to give the doctor an earful.

I believe she had to tell someone of her distrust of me with hopes that someone would sympathize with her. I didn't have the medical training to understand her intense distrust. I thought things would never be the same ever again. I was having difficulty taking the verbal abuse.

As I'm writing about Elaine's futile fight with Alzheimer's, I'm beginning to feel as if I'm actually reliving the past seven years. I never imagined that recalling the past would impact me to the degree it has. Up to this point, my trials and tribulations had not been discussed with the family. Those times are best left alone. I only hope our story will help you recognize adverse behavior and provide you with a better understanding of what to expect and how to cope with your loved one's challenges. Whatever happens, always be there for the person you love because your love and care may be all they have left.

Earlier in this book, I mentioned Elaine's occasional displays of incredible strength. There was another incident when she displayed that strength. Early one evening, she was very upset and complained of pain in her stomach. I suggested we go the hospital emergency room and have them check it out. She refused to go and wouldn't put on her coat. When I tried to help her, she got violently angry. I called Tom for help and the two of us could not control her. Her strength was unbelievable and I threatened to call the police and ambulance. Actually, it was not a threat; we needed help. When she heard me mention an ambulance she relented and allowed us to take her to the hospital. Care-givers should be aware of the unusual show of strength displayed by Alzheimer's victims when they are in a determined state of mind.

Early one morning around 1:30 AM Elaine made several attempts to leave the house. She kept saying that she "wanted to get out of here." I finally lost my patience and told her to put on her coat. I was going to show her places where she may be happier. I drove past three different assisted living facilities and asked which one she would like to stay at. I stopped at one facility and told her I would go to the door and see if she could move in immediately. I knew this was a mean thing to do. I was so desperate I just wanted to settle her down and get some sleep. The threat obviously frightened her. She behaved the rest of the night and we both got some much-needed rest.

The very next day Elaine again made several attempts to leave the house. Getting her to settle down seemed as difficult as getting a raging bull to be gentle. I was running out of ideas to distract her and tried to think of anything that may spark her interest. Then I remembered how Craig had once diverted her attention by jokingly putting an extra piece of bacon on her plate at breakfast. She never realized what he had done, but it seemed to calm her.

At this point, anything was worth trying and it seemed I may be able to control her unpredictable behavior by changing her focus. I offered a snack, cup of tea, ice cream or anything I thought of. This method did work some of the time and it was an improvement.

Elaine's Alzheimer's was aggravated by her limited mobility. She was having difficulty getting into bed and she needed help lifting her legs onto the bed. This made it very difficult for her to get into a comfortable position for sleep. The fact that she was always cold didn't make things any easier. She wore sweats to bed which made it troublesome to move under the covers. I couldn't convince her that wearing less clothing would stop her clothes clutching to the bedding.

I was beginning to notice changes in my own demeanor. Because of the circumstances I was awake most nights. Something had to change and I didn't have a solution in mind. I reached out for help and my son Craig offered to come over and stay the night so that I could get some rest. He did, but I still remained aware of Elaine's movements throughout the night. This arrangement didn't relieve me of my anxiety and I didn't want Craig to be inconvenienced. He was disappointed when I told him I would take care of the matter myself.

A few months later, my family thought it would be a good idea to hire temporary help. They called a woman to come over for an interview. Tom, Mark and Lori were there to help me determine if she would be acceptable. Elaine came into the living room, surmised what was going on and negatively voiced her opinion. After the woman left Elaine continued to express her objections to having another woman in her house. This should have been a predictable response because of her suspicions of my infidelity. Needless to say, the idea went by the wayside.

CHAPTER 7

"It's time."

I TOOK ELAINE to the doctor for a checkup. Her behavior was out of control and I needed ideas fast. It was at this visit that Dr. Hettrick simply said, "It's time." Those were the dreaded words I prayed I would never hear. He was a man of few words, but his message came through loud and clear. I knew then our lives would change forever.

I had visited various facilities in Kenosha and the surrounding area. These were primarily for assisted living and were not suitable for us. I also found that at an assisted living facility the patient was financially responsible for the first two years of care. This was a surprising revelation. The projected cost of annual care for Elaine, exceeded our annual income. Unbeknownst to me, my family members were looking for a place that specifically cared for Alzheimer's patients. They were focusing on facilities that had lock-down capabilities.

As I was considering confining Elaine in a nursing facility, I made inquiries with the ADRC about any financial aid we might be eligible for. Asking a lot of questions, particularly about specific requirements was the most important thing I could have done. It made me aware of everything needed to correctly complete the application for assistance. The ADRC provided an application and I began gathering the necessary information for approval.

The amount of personal and financial information required completely stripped away our privacy. One should expect to dedicate a great deal of time gathering the necessary data for these applications. If there is any indication that your circumstance may involve financial aid, I strongly suggest you start your research now.

On a Saturday morning in late April, 2016, Tom and I visited several nursing homes that Tom's wife, Bonnie, thought suitable for Elaine. After some serious consideration, we decided on a nursing home that was located just 15 minutes from our house. I didn't have any idea what part I would play in caring for Elaine in the facility. But, when I settled into a routine, living near the nursing home was a definite advantage.

I had an appointment with my Dermatologist the following Monday and Lori stayed with Elaine at home. The doctor removed some suspicious tissue from the top of my head and submitted it for a biopsy. I soon received a call informing me that the biopsy indicated cancer. While still on the phone, I made an appointment to have a surgical procedure to remove the cancer.

The procedure was done on the Thursday before Mother's Day. I was given specific instructions for post-operative care of the affected area and, when the doctor finished and put a band aid on my head, I asked her if my hair would prevent the band aid from adhering to my head. She said that was not an issue. It was a nice way of telling me I was bald. Actually, I already knew that.

Caring for Elaine was more than a full-time job. My attention was primarily focused on her and I was becoming overwhelmed with details of her care and my own. My judgement was slipping. As a result, I misread the instructions on the tube of my medication. On the tube itself, I quickly read to stop application after 3 days. However, the written instructions from the doctor indicated the medication was to be applied twice daily, continuously. My not taking the time to verify the instructions resulted in a lengthy healing process. I wasn't sure if the doctor would have a solution to overcome the damage that resulted from my impatience.

Mother's Day 2016 was the following Sunday. Because of Elaine's unpredictable condition I didn't plan any formal gathering for the family. Everyone came to visit and all brought flowers. Jim was unable to make the trip from Nashville, but he sent flowers that arrived earlier.

The mention of flowers brought to mind a story I would like to share here. Years earlier, we lived in a Chicago suburb and I worked downtown. I left for work one morning in a bad mood and left the house without saying goodbye to Elaine. I felt guilty all day and kept thinking about how I could apologize. As I left the building a vendor was standing nearby selling floral bouquets. This was the first time I ever bought Elaine flowers and I thought they would be a great peace offering. I bought two bouquets and confidently went home.

Armed with the flowers, I briskly walked into the house and presented them to her. Without hesitation she said, "What did you do wrong?" After that experience, I never did anything out of the ordinary again. Flowers were definitely off the list.

The day after Mother's Day, Elaine was having a difficult time. She was restless and continuously wandered around the house. I didn't shadow her every move, I simply listened for any signs of distress. That evening she refused to go upstairs to bed. After several attempts to persuade her, I relented and decided that I had no choice but to stay with her on the first floor. I had to make sure she didn't try to get up the stairs in the night and the only way for me to do this was to sleep on the floor at the foot of the stairs. The ceramic tile was very cold and uncomfortable, so I placed a carpet runner and a heavy blanket on the floor. I didn't fall into a deep sleep and occasionally heard Elaine running water in the kitchen and powder room. In my half-sleep I didn't feel any cause for alarm. But at about 4:30 AM, I decided to see if she was having any problems.

I was flabbergasted! Elaine had taken all the flowers she received on Mother's Day and had them in total disarray on the counters and the floor in the kitchen and powder room. The sink in the powder room was plugged with whatever it was she tried to drain. I had no choice but to retrieve my tools from the basement and take the plumbing apart to fix the sink drain. This could not happen again so I decided the best solution would be to shut off the water supply valves under the sinks. When I knelt down and reached under the counter, I struck my head directly on the spot of the cancer surgery. The pain was excruciating and I let loose a few expletives. "Why me and what else could possibly go wrong?"

After cleaning the mess of the flowers and water spills, I took Elaine upstairs. She didn't resist. I remembered hearing that a person with Alzheimer's is capable of sensing one's demeanor. She probably picked up on my total frustration and knew I wouldn't tolerate any nonsense.

When I submitted the application for financial aid for Elaine's facility, I was told the process could take up to 3 months and I should expect at least one rejection. Fortunately, the gentleman who assisted me with the application was an employee of the nursing home we selected and he told me precisely what was required to qualify for assistance. I followed his instructions and we received a letter of approval within 15 days. It is extremely important that if you submit an application for financial aid, be honest with your declaration of assets. I always believed that a liar must have a good memory. The truth is always the same and therefore doesn't require a good memory.

I went to the facility to present the final approval documentation. When leaving the building, I took a few steps and stopped. The implications of committing Elaine to this institution hit me full-force. I just stood there and cried. I immediately had doubts about what I had done and didn't know how I could live with myself. The guilt was almost too much to bear. I dreaded the thought of having to face Elaine and pretend all was well. It was a very dark day in our lives together. A few days later I received a call from the nursing home informing me of an admission date of May 20, 2016. Craig offered to be with me when I took Elaine to the facility.

CHAPTER 8

—— ❧ ——

The Dreaded Day

It was May 20th and it would be the day that changed our lives forever. Elaine was scheduled to arrive at the facility at 10:30 AM. Craig was with us and the drive was somber. When I looked at Elaine she looked like a sheep being led to slaughter. She didn't have a clue as to the fate awaiting her. The compassion I felt for her was overwhelming and I began to question my decision to confine her in an institution for the rest of her life.

When we arrived, she asked me where we were; I told her she was at a place that would take care of her and keep her safe. We went in and the young lady from admissions was waiting for us. She led us to the second floor which housed the lockdown facility. She pressed a red entry button and Elaine refused to enter. After some persuasion, she relented and we proceeded to her room. The room was typical of most facilities I had visited. There was a single bed, dresser, closet, TV, private sink and a chair or two.

We were invited to make the room as homey as we wished and my first concern was to make her comfortable. I helped remove her coat and Craig hung it in the closet with the rest of her clothes. She sat on the bed and was very confused being in an unfamiliar environment. I tried to assure her that she was in a safe place and this was her new home. She wasn't entirely convinced but didn't ask any more about it.

She wore a gold pendant on a gold chain that she cherished more than any other piece of jewelry she owned. The pendant was about the size of a silver dollar and had a raised replica of her birth sign, which was a crab. She was also wearing two rings. I heard horror stories about attendants at nursing facilities taking valuable items from patients and decided to remove the necklace. She became hysterical. It didn't make any sense for her to be in such distress because of a piece of jewelry. I placed it back around her neck and she immediately calmed down. I also left the rings on her fingers.

The medallion was gone within 10 days and the rings lasted about 3 weeks. I don't blame or hold any animosity toward anyone for the loss of her jewelry. I don't fault anyone at the nursing home. It's best to leave it at that. I was criticized for leaving those items and I simply reiterated how insignificant a personal possession was at a time like that.

A nurse came in to give Elaine a preliminary once over; we settled her in and left. I previously mentioned encountering dark days during Elaine's Alzheimer's journey; I can't categorize any one day as being the darkest. They are too numerous to mention. However, looking back, I'm sure this day would be remembered as the darkest of our lives. Craig and I drove home without much conversation. I know this incident affected him tremendously and I thanked him for his support.

I was informed that it would take at least two weeks before Elaine would become acclimated with her new surroundings and it was advised that I allow it to happen. I understood that to mean it would be best if I stayed away. It was Thursday when she entered the nursing home and it has been over six years since Elaine and I have been apart.

On Sunday, I called longtime friends, Joe and Mary in Huntsville, Alabama. Elaine and I had known them since 1957 and asked if I could visit. They encouraged me to come down and we arranged for a visit on the following Tuesday. I felt a need to get away and wanted to take my time driving while contemplating our future. Normally the drive can be done in one day. I took my time and arrived in two days. We had a reciprocal understanding with these friends. When they visit up north they're welcome in our home and when we travel south we're welcome in theirs.

I arrived on Tuesday afternoon and told our friends what had transpired. I called the nursing home the next morning to ask how Elaine was. I happened to call the dining room at lunch time and the young lady on the phone told me she was fine and would I like to talk to her? I didn't realize I could bother her and, of course, immediately agreed. When Elaine got on the phone we both started to cry and between the sobbing I told her I would be there early the next morning. I placed the call at 11:45 AM and was on my way home at 12:00 PM. I arrived in Kenosha at 10:30 PM.

It took Elaine quite a while to fully adjust to her new home. My new lifestyle was simple. I arrived at the facility at approximately 7:15 AM and stayed with her until after lunch. Arriving early gave me an opportunity to get her ready for the day. The first order of business was to brush her teeth, pretend to clean the insignificant hair from her chin, wash her and put the hot washcloth on her face.

At the beginning of her stay, everything was going along fine. She was responsive and didn't give me any trouble. I learned about "Sundowner's Syndrome" and its profound effect on most Alzheimer's patients. This was a perfect name for the anomaly because it generally occurred in the late afternoon. Because I usually went home in the early afternoons, I only experienced the phenomenon on a few occasions when I either stayed late or returned in the late afternoon.

My concern about Sundowner's Syndrome or "Sundowning," led me to do some research on the matter. Prior to Elaine being admitted Sundowner's Syndrome was seldom mentioned and only in a passive way. There are many changes in behavior that can take place during the sun downing period, which generally occurs just before dark. As a caregiver of someone who has Alzheimer's or another form of dementia you may notice that they become more confused or agitated in the late afternoon or at twilight.

It seems that the Sundowners symptoms may have something to do with late day darkness. Some of the changes in behavior that I experienced with Elaine during the sundowning period were anger, stubbornness, fear, violence, anxiety and crying. She also feared for my safety and would tell me to be careful. When I would tell her not to worry, she would be more emphatic about her concern for my safety. I could never understand why she was so concerned about me but I could only try to reassure her that I would be alright.

My son Craig noticed that asking an Alzheimer's patient questions would often trigger a negative response. Negative in the sense that asking would create an atmosphere of confusion for the patient. It was more productive to have a conversation that didn't require any answers.

Elaine's facility had a laundry service which was offered as part of the program. I marked her clothes with her name and was told that everything would be distributed to her properly. The amount of laundry the facility generated every day was staggering.

There were occasions when Elaine's laundry was delayed in returning and I went to the laundry room to see if I could locate any of her clothes. Eventually, I decided it would be best if I took her clothes home to be laundered. But I had a hard time conveying this to the facility, probably because there were several people that watched over the patients. I spoke with the administrator and asked if I could tape a sign to the closet door indicating that her family does the laundry and that a hamper for soiled cloths was in the closet. My request was approved and the sign was posted.

Most of the staff respected my wishes, but occasionally her cloths were still sent to the laundry. As a result of that, I went to the laundry almost every day to look for something she was missing and became well known to the laundry personnel. They were very patient with me and after a short time almost everyone at the home knew me and Elaine. Over a period of time Elaine was missing jackets, shoes and blankets. This also was something I had no control over and rather than blame anyone I simply accepted it as part of life in a nursing home and let it go. I discovered that the patients would go into other's rooms and take clothing and shoes. On one occasion, another patient rolled into Elaine's room, pointed to the clothes in the closet and informed me that they were hers. I just said, "OK" and let it go. I'm a firm believer in that if you acquire something in a dishonest manner, you will never enjoy what you have taken.

CHAPTER 9

⚬

A Different Environment

LONG BEFORE ELAINE entered the nursing home our sons decided to appoint one of them as liaison to convey any news of Elaine or other things related to the family. By doing this, they avoided any repetition or confusion about a new course of action. Tom, the eldest, was designated the task. If I had any news I thought the family should be aware of, I simply told Tom and the message was relayed.

Through their grapevine, they put together a plan to have everyone prepare meals for us that could be frozen and kept for use as needed. This was a tremendous help to me and eliminated the need to prepare all the meals. With their contributions and my supplemental cooking, there was never a need for additional food. When they periodically asked if we needed more food, I told them it wasn't necessary. I discovered at a much later date that my family was doing much more behind the scenes than I realized. I credit Elaine for instilling that family bond in our sons.

I'm sure we have all experienced stormy relationships in our lives, particularly amongst siblings. That was the case with our five boys. As always, the misunderstandings would be resolved and in the end, no one was successful in destroying the bond between the brothers. However, there were some that tried with a vengeance. They are no longer a part of our family.

Now that Elaine was situated in a safe place, I was able to contact a friend from the Coast Guard Auxiliary and arrange to meet for breakfast. After taking care of Elaine and getting her ready for breakfast, I told her I would be back soon. I was probably gone for about one and a half hours. When I returned there were several staff members standing at the nurse's station engaged in girl talk.

As I walked in, I happened to look to my left and saw Elaine in an unoccupied room lying on the floor in the corner of the room. She could not be seen from the nurse's station and no one saw her fall. She was lucid and not calling for help. Two of nurses rushed into the room with me and we carefully helped her to her feet. She wasn't injured nor did she show any signs of distress. She and I walked to her room and talked. She couldn't express her thoughts to me very well, but it was clear that she didn't remember falling.

I couldn't bring myself to really trust others to care for Elaine. It was much more comforting for me to control as much of her day as possible. This may have been an unobtainable goal, because her activities were unknown to me from midafternoon until the following morning. Mark visited quite often, sometimes in the late afternoon. He told me stories about his encounters with Sundowners Syndrome and was surprised at the effect it had on the patients. He was very compassionate with the other patients in the ward. I don't believe Mark ever passed a person without acknowledging them. That's a remarkable attribute to be blessed with.

There were times when Elaine was very aware of her surroundings. One day I left and she was standing by the window and saw me getting into the car. She pointed toward me and said to a staff member, "Look at that SOB! He's leaving." At that moment she seemed to know what she was saying, and didn't seem to give it any further thought. That was another quirk of Alzheimer's that was repeated several times in the future.

We often walked back and forth in the corridor and dining area. She was pretty steady while walking and it was good exercise for both of us. It also provided an opportunity to leave her room for a change of scenery. It was a good way of mingling and getting acquainted with the other patients.

Patients were weighed every month, and Elaine lost about ten pounds the first month. There wasn't a concern and her weight loss was attributed to the adjustment to her new environment. I kept notes on all of her statistics, especially her medications. She was annoyed with the chronic pain in her legs. I asked that something be prescribed to alleviate or at least make the pain manageable. They contacted her doctor and started a regimen of a pain reliever. The dosage was adjusted to a level that helped her cope.

After being in the facility for a while, it became apparent that Elaine needed a different type of clothing. The slacks, blouses and light jackets from home were not easy to maintain, and Lori was kind enough to help me shop for wrinkle free, soft clothing. She also considered the ease of washing, folding and transporting the clothes. The fabrics were such that folding and packing had no effect on the appearance. Since I was doing the laundry and didn't have to separate the items in the washer, the chore was almost a pleasure. Almost, being the key word.

Dressing Elaine was a challenge and has been even while she was still at home. There weren't many changes in the morning routine at the facility, except that we both had to adjust to the free-standing sink outside the toilet room. There was no countertop and I utilized a food serving table near the sink to help get her clean and ready for the day.

When placed in an unfamiliar situation, you become attuned to the underlying activities around you. Every morning I would assume the responsibility of getting Elaine ready for the day. But, there were mornings when she needed immediate help. She may have wet herself or fell while trying to get out of bed. Rather than call for assistance I would take care of the problem myself. This was the norm until I had a discussion with a staff member, who shared with me that she overheard another staff member say, "Don't worry about Elaine, her husband will take care of her."

I thought of the possibility of that happening but never considered that it would. From that moment on everything changed. Every morning I asked for assistance and soon after, Elaine was awake and dressed before I arrived. I never reported the incident to the management. Since I wasn't able to be with Elaine 24 hours a day, these staff members were my lifeline and I didn't want to upset the apple cart.

Elaine's mobility was limited, but she was able to move about and join the others in the dining room for daily activities. She enjoyed playing a game in which everyone sat in a circle trying to hit a balloon and preventing it from hitting the floor. She played with a great deal of enthusiasm and it was fun to watch her engross herself in the activity. There were coloring books and drawing materials available and even though she could draw very well, she didn't take any interest in using the materials provided. Her ability to concentrate was very limited and she would change from one thought to another in an instant.

Elaine was a very giving person. It wasn't unusual for her to help another patient before worrying about herself. Several times I saw her approach a person who seemed distressed, put her arms around them and simply hold them for a few minutes. Once, I noticed that she hugged a woman who was holding her head in her hands in distress. Soon, the woman began to smile and gently touched Elaine. She complimented the staff. If someone told her she looked beautiful, she would always return the compliment.

A few of the patients were capable of light conversation and were pretty astute in sharing their thoughts. Elaine wasn't able to carry on a conversation with any clarity at all. However, when she talked to someone it never ceased to amaze me how they understood what she was trying to say. Even when plagued with the effects of their illnesses, they somehow knew what the other was thinking. This may be similar to what happens to a blind or deaf person. The remaining senses seem to be much more sensitive and automatically compensate for the loss.

One of the male patients was enamored with Elaine. We often sat with him at breakfast or lunch and he would always ask me if he could say something. Of course, I said "yes" and he would always compliment Elaine by telling her she had a beautiful smile or very nice-looking hair. This happened at almost every meal.

There were several others we visited with at meal time or while walking around. The limitations of the others soon became apparent and I always spoke to them in simple terms. One woman insisted that I stole her embroidered pillow and confronted me about the theft incessantly. Nothing I said would convince her otherwise so I told her it was in her room. That ploy worked for a while and she became amicable again and would engage me in simple conversation. Soon after, her suspicions would return and the process would start all over again. I often had to remind myself of the cognitive limitations suffered by these poor souls.

I tried to find humor in the situation. One man would stand guard outside his room and swear at passersby. I knew he didn't mean any harm, but I always kept a lot of distance between us. The patient's behaviors were very unpredictable, so I always adhered to the old adage, "better safe than sorry."

I remember one woman in particular that moved into the facility. She looked like a lost soul on her first day in the dining room. I wanted to make her feel at home and invited her to sit with Elaine and me. She asked our names, we had some light moments of laughter and we enjoyed her company. It wasn't long after that she seemed to change. She didn't mingle with the others and wasn't able to sit long enough to finish her meals. I guess she was too nervous to relax. That, of course, is a very non-professional observation.

There were many others in the ward and most were very pleasant. The one thing most had in common was their strong desire to leave. The alarmed doors kept most patients safe inside, but if someone did leave the ward, it only took a few moments to find them. They were usually found across the hall near the nurse's desk. One man would always sit by the nurse's desk at the entrance. When asked how everything was, he would tell you his mother was sick and he wanted to leave. It was either that, or he was waiting for someone to pick him up. He was prepared to walk home to Waukegan if they didn't arrive. Then he would ask if I knew where Waukegan was. Sadly, that was his whole world.

Everyone had a story and a life before the facility. When I looked at the emptiness and frustration of these people's faces I couldn't help but wonder what purpose our creator had in mind for these poor souls. Perhaps it's natural to harbor such questions without being sacrilegious. I don't know the answer and accept the fact that I never will.

About two weeks into her stay, Elaine did not seem stressed when I left. She rarely got hysterical anymore and she settled down shortly after I would leave. There were very few occasions when she asked me not to leave or said that she wanted to go with me. I was always grateful for that. It would have made it very difficult if it were any other way. Soon, she was so unaffected by me leaving that when we walked to the exit near the nurse's station, I would kiss her goodbye and she would just turn around and walk away.

Elaine was troubled by shaking in her right hand. It wasn't a violent movement, and at the beginning of her stay at the facility it didn't greatly affect her ability to eat. The only help she required from me was to cut solid foods. Although it was difficult for her to open various condiment containers, if she persisted she was successful.

During the first two or three weeks, I wasn't aware that I could purchase meals and have lunch with Elaine. I took advantage of the service and in so doing I eliminated the need to prepare meals for myself at home. When she was at home we generally ate two meals a day with a light snack in the late afternoon. Having lunch with Elaine made my day much easier.

My new daily routine was fairly simple. I arrived at the nursing home at about 7:15 AM, left between 1:30 PM and 3:00 PM, went home to do the laundry, folded the clothes and packed them for the next day. There was always enough soiled clothing to require daily laundry chores. After the chores, I relaxed with my computer and watched TV until it was time to retire.

It wasn't a very exciting existence, but at the time I never gave it any thought. My family was concerned and tried to diversify my time with suggestions of taking a day off and doing something for myself. I honestly didn't feel the need nor did I want to do anything alone. I just wanted to be with Elaine. Even when she seemed completely lost in thought, I knew she was aware of my presence.

We were told that it was acceptable to bring items to make her room as homey as possible. Mark brought several pictures and hung them on the walls. He also wrote some of Elaine's favorite quotes and put those on the wall. One of her favorites was, "Let go and let God."

The seating in the room was sparse and I purchased a recliner and large chair. Elaine was inclined to sleep in the recliner rather than bed. This furniture was upholstered and, when I purchased it, I wasn't thinking about keeping the fabric clean and sanitary. I found out soon enough after I cleaned the chair with Lysol a few times. The furniture had to go.

I had the chair cleaned and sanitized and gave it to the nursing home with the hope that someone would make good use of it. I was surprised how grateful they were to receive the chair and they informed me that many of the patients didn't have any amenities. It was almost as though they were dropped off at the front door and forgotten. I cannot imagine anyone living their final years or days without any support from family or a friend. I did replace the furniture with vinyl upholstered chairs. This was much easier to keep clean and sanitary. Now that I think about, buying the cloth furniture wasn't very smart.

At one point, I contacted Hospice and they agreed to monitor Elaine as a facility patient. A nurse visited once a week and they also provided ministry and counseling service. A young woman came in three times a week to help Elaine shower. Having Hospice care proved to be very beneficial. It gave me an opportunity to monitor Elaine's medication intake and any changes were made directly and immediately through Hospice. Her doctor was affiliated with Hospice and the direct contact eliminated issues that could have possibly delayed any decisions regarding her care. When her doctor visited he checked her as if it were an office visit. Hospice also provided a very comfortable bed and a wheel-chair. When Elaine began the Hospice program, she had no need for the wheel-chair. However, it was an invaluable addition later in her stay.

One thing I remember clearly from this time was when a young lady came into Elaine's room with a guitar and sang a few tunes. She was very good and I thought it was great for Elaine since she always liked music. I told Elaine how much I enjoyed the entertainment. To my surprise, she told me she didn't want her to come back.

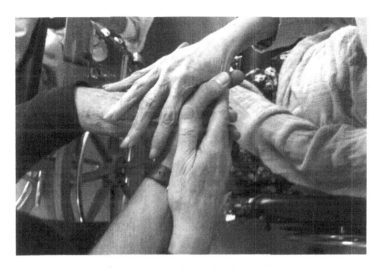

Elaine consoling other nursing home patients

CHAPTER 10

Rapid Decline

I BEGAN TO notice a marked regression in Elaine's speech, and at times I couldn't understand her. I acknowledged what she said by uttering something. If my utterance was positive and should have been negative or vice versa, she would get upset. I now had to respond with a generic sound a non-committal tone. This worked well and eliminated her frustration.

Her inability to communicate fluctuated. There were moments when she was fairly understandable. This usually happened when she had a visitor, particularly if it was someone she hadn't seen for a long time. Because I spent so much time with Elaine, I was used to her manner of speaking. I gave some serious thought about her increased ability to express herself with those she saw only occasionally. I worried that I was the one who made her uncomfortable.

My mind was put at ease when I learned that many of my family members felt the same way. As a care-giver, you may also question your reactions to new situations. If you can't resolve an issue, don't hesitate to ask for help. There is often a simple remedy to what may seem to be a huge roadblock.

One morning, I arrived in Elaine's room and, when I opened the door she was on the floor on her hands and knees. While getting out of bed she leaned forward to get up, leaned too far and fell forward. I helped her up, made sure she wasn't injured and sat with her on the bed until she relaxed. I never showed any alarm. As the father of five boys, I learned over the years that, when they were hurt, it was best to show no distress. By remaining calm the one hurt also minimizes the injury. That philosophy also worked with Elaine every time.

Six months passed before I came to the realization that Elaine would never come home. I decided to give her clothes away and Lori helped me determine how to distribute everything. The amount of Elaine's clothing was staggering and we spent almost three hours clearing the closets. Whatever Lori decided not to save for herself or the granddaughters was donated to a charitable organization. Looking at the now-empty closets was no less painful then when her clothes were in sight.

One morning as I walked toward the facility entrance I abruptly stopped and wondered to myself if I could continue to care for Elaine any longer. The regimen was wearing me down; I had to find a way to go on. That evening while watching ROKU and scrolling through programs, I saw a description that looked very interesting about a woman who said that God had whispered something in her ear. My curiosity won over and I couldn't pass that by without finding what it was that God had whispered. She revealed that He said, "the strong must remain strong so that they may help the weak." I'm not a preacher, but I think everyone believes or should believe in a higher power. It doesn't matter what name we give that power, it's only important that we place our faith and trust in it. That message made complete sense to me and it gave me a reason to go on. If I ever doubted my ability to continue the fight for Elaine, I thought about those powerful whispered words. It is remarkable how help comes to you if you're hopeful and receptive.

Jim drove up from Nashville, stayed with Craig for the night and planned to visit Elaine in the morning. They stopped for breakfast at a place that also baked and sold sweet rolls. Jim purchased ten sweet rolls for the caregivers at the home and almost fainted when the bill was $50.00 plus tax. On the way to the home they picked up Craig's son Christopher and his three-year-old daughter Rhiannon. When they arrived, Elaine was in the dining room. One of the patients was confined to a wheelchair and had the bad habit of stealing food from other patients while they weren't looking. Jim placed the box of sweet rolls on the desk counter and, as soon as Jim's back was turned, the box was in the hands of the wheelchair thief. Christopher told me that watching his uncle engaged in a tug of war over a box of sweet rolls with an old man in a wheel chair was the most hilarious thing he had ever seen. That incident remains one of the lighter highlights of our memories.

Elaine was blessed with an abundance of visitors. My sister Trudy, several of our grandchildren, great- grandchildren, family and friends visited Elaine. Craig's daughter Jillian and her husband Veto came with their daughters Gia and Lillyanna. Craig's son Christopher came with his wife Anna and daughter Rhiannon. Jim brought his daughter Jessica. John's son Jason visited with his son Cameron. Mark and Lori came with sons David, James and Michael and cousin "little" Nancy.

Elaine was always in a happy mood when the grandchildren came to see her. She seemed to relax and treasure every moment. Her best friend Elaine visited with her daughter Kelly and those visits meant a great deal to her.

She recognized people she hadn't seen in years. Once, a former daughter-in law, Cathy visited. When she arrived, we were standing in the corridor just outside her room. Her room was near the dining area which was at the farthest distance from the entrance at the nurse's station. Elaine saw her and immediately recognized her, called her by name and started to cry. It was amazing to witness this because her cognitive skills were so diminished. This happened a few other times and it is a good example of person's being able to recall things from the past but not the present.

The family visited on a regular basis. When Mark visited he would occasionally bring his dog, Sadie. She was very small and loved people. The patients were very excited to have her visit and they couldn't get enough of her. They would all pet her and some wanted to hold her. Sadie's presence never failed to brighten the day. Mark occasionally treated the care-givers to a pizza or fried chicken lunch. There was always enough for the staff on both wings. They appreciated the recognition of their dedication. Mark generally visited just before lunch and sometimes in the late afternoon. It gave me comfort to know that Elaine had visits from loved ones after I went home for the day.

A television and CD player were available in the dining room. Music was provided during lunch and I brought several CD's from home. The music was a great tranquilizer and on more than one occasion Elaine asked me to dance. It was wonderful to hold her in my arms again. Of course, it was always a slow dance, but just to feel her melt in my arms was more than I ever imagined possible again.

Mark was visiting Elaine one late afternoon when she asked him to dance. He said she put her head on his shoulder and called him "Con." Her favorite song was "More." The first part of the lyric was, "More than the greatest love the world has known," Believe it or not, as I wrote this, I was crying like a fool. Elaine and I had taken ballroom dancing lessons many years prior and always took advantage of the opportunity to dance at weddings and parties. Because I was an officer of a corporation, we were often invited to attend various business functions that offered dinner and dancing. Dancing with Elaine was one of the things I missed the most. Those were the moments when we could be alone amongst a crowd of people.

My sons began pleading with me to take a day off and enjoy myself. I took their advice and planned to visit a friend. It was about 11:00 AM and I had just entered the interstate in Kenosha. I suddenly got a strong feeling that I should go to Elaine's facility. I followed my instincts and turned off at the first exit. When I entered the ward, a CNA told me that Elaine had fallen in the dining room and asked how I got there so fast. She was walking with a walker when the wheel caught on a chair and threw her off balance.

An ambulance was summoned and I arrived before the medics. While falling, she struck her head on a cabinet and landed on her back. She was disoriented and I couldn't do any more than reassure her I was there for her and everything would be fine. She was taken to the hospital where they checked her condition and determined it was safe to release her. It was lunch time and we went to a fried chicken restaurant and enjoyed a quiet meal.

Once, I did actually take a day off to visit my 93-tear-old sister Trudy in Elk Grove, IL. It's about an hour drive from Kenosha. Trudy prepared a nice lunch, we talked a while and I left in mid-afternoon to avoid north bound rush hour traffic. As I approached the Kenosha exits I decided to stop in and have dinner with Elaine.

For weeks, Elaine had been having a terrible problem with itchy skin. We tried various lotions, one of which was recommended by my Dermatologist, and a prescription drug. Nothing seemed to help. She didn't understand that the itching wouldn't be as severe if she didn't scratch. I applied lotion as part of preparing her for the day. Lori applied the lotion when she visited in the afternoon.

It was during one of these visits that Elaine asked Lori to contact a lawyer so she could divorce me. The strangest thing and the most difficult to accept was that Elaine loved me and despised me at the same time. When I left in the afternoon I always asked if she liked me. She would always say, "I love you," and I would tell her, "I love you too, baby."

Conrad and Elaine, dancing at various functions

CHAPTER 11

—— ✽ ——

The Inevitable

ELAINE WAS DECLINING rapidly. For example, she no longer knew what I wanted when I asked her to remove her upper plate for cleaning. The tooth brush had to be put in her hand and put up to her mouth for her to brush her teeth. When leaving the bathroom, I had to direct her to stand by the sink to wash her hands.

She wasn't able to feed herself and her food consumption had diminished. Her tastes were changing from liking something one day and refusing to eat the same thing the next. Her mobility had also declined and she used a wheelchair on a regular basis.

For months, Elaine had preferred sleeping in the lounge chair, but now she was spending more time in her bed. It took a long time for her to wake up in the morning and get ready for breakfast. She often walked with her eyes closed and I had a difficult time convincing her to open them so she could see where she was going. When exiting room, she didn't know which way to turn and I had to direct her toward the dining room. I fed her breakfast, returned to the room, took her to the bathroom, put her in the lounge chair and covered her with a light blanket. In a very short time she would be asleep. I knew her behavior indicated further decline.

One morning I arrived and noticed Elaine's teeth were missing and she didn't know where they were. After a frantic search I found her plate under some folding chairs. Two days later, I found her teeth under the bed. When it happened a third time in four days I realized that something needed to be done. I had a dental appointment the following day and I asked the dentist if a dental plate could be made using the original as a template. The technician verified that this could be done and I took her plate that same afternoon, had a new plate made and returned with a spare, just in case.

My concern was that, if she lost her teeth, it would be impossible for her to go to the dentist and sit long enough to have impressions made. I couldn't imagine Elaine having to eat without being able to chew. It was bad enough that her dinner that night consisted of food that looked as if it came out of a baby food jar. Two patients in the ward had their meals mashed because they were unable to chew. With all the patients' other problems, eating needn't be another one.

Elaine was eating less and sleeping more. During this late stage, she had no control of her legs and arms and they constantly moved in a jerking motion. As a result of the movement she had difficulty remaining in one position. She was unable to communicate at all and I could only guess how I could make her comfortable.

The Monday after I had the new plate made, a Hospice nurse came for a visit. She looked at Elaine and told me she had "terminal restlessness." I didn't question her about her diagnosis. She proceeded to check Elaine's vitals, explained Elaine's condition and left. The next day a different Hospice nurse arrived, looked at Elaine, and also pronounced "terminal restlessness." This time, the word "terminal" peaked my curiosity and I asked her if that meant Elaine only had a few months.

She told me it could possibly be weeks or as little as one week. My heart sank. The end was near and there was nothing I could do to change it.

For the remainder of the week, I brought Elaine's meals to her room. That provided privacy and she wasn't burdened with getting into the wheelchair. When Saturday arrived, the restlessness was much more pronounced. I called a few family members and told them it was time.

Craig had said from the beginning that he wanted to be with Elaine when she passed. Unfortunately, he was in Florida and Mark was on vacation in Mexico Both were unable to arrive soon enough. Our god daughter Kelly and several grandchildren arrived to be with Elaine. Craig's daughter Jillian sat on a chair talking to Elaine and wetting her lips with a small sponge. Her legs and arms were moving up and down and she seemed more comfortable with her legs against the wall.

We could not get her into a position comfortable enough for her to stop moving. I called for a priest and he administered last rights. It was midafternoon and since there was nothing more to be done, I asked everyone to leave. Kelly had driven from Frankfort, IL and I was concerned for her safety. We left together about 4:30 PM. I went home to eat and returned to the facility at 6:00 PM. I wanted to be sure she was securely tucked into bed and I left for the day.

The next day was a Sunday and I returned at about 7:00 AM. When I arrived, I went into Elaine's room and she was lying on her back perfectly still, with her arms at her side, breathing with her mouth open with oxygen being administered through her nose.

She was totally unaware and the only response I got was a pursing of her lips when I gently placed some water near her mouth. She was obviously dying and I could only talk to her and tell her how much we all loved her. I kept talking because I had heard that, even in that condition, the dying can still hear. I only had two prayer requests in my entire life: that I remain healthy enough to raise my family and that Elaine dies before me. That may seem selfish but I don't believe she would have been able to take care of herself and I know she wouldn't want to be a burden to our sons.

Mark's son James called and asked if he could come and keep me company. He arrived at about 9:00 AM. This was his first experience witnessing a person dying and I believe it had a profound and positive effect on him.

The nurse was putting a drop of morphine on Elaine's tongue periodically and when I stroked Elaine's head I noticed it was warm. I asked the nurse and she put a cold wash cloth on her forehead. I continued to tell her nice things and finally told her I would be alright if she wanted to go. A few minutes later she was gone.

I knew the exact moment she died. It was 10:30 AM on Sunday, January 22, 2017. It was almost exactly sixty-four years, four months and two days into our marriage. I called the nurse and she made all the necessary contacts and I called the mortician. The time of death was pronounced by the hospice nurse as 11:30 AM.

James wasn't in the room when Elaine passed but he knew something happened when he saw the commotion outside her room. He helped me notify family members and, after the mortician was finished, we left. When I walked out that door, I left half my life behind me.

Despair, 12/2016

❧

CHAPTER 12

Everything Changes

ELAINE AND I had talked about our wishes for our last services and burials. We both wanted to be cremated and have unobtrusive memorial services. I did not place an obituary in the newspaper and the memorial service was for family only. I opted to forego a funeral procession, and, when the priest mentioned taking the remains to the cemetery from the church, I asked him to arrange the burial for a future date.

We went from the church service directly to the restaurant for lunch. The memorial service was on the Saturday after she passed and the burial service was conducted on the following Tuesday at 10:00 AM. Our sons Jim, John and Craig along with Mark's wife Lori and I were at the burial service.

A good friend of mine is Jewish and I learned that they traditionally visit the surviving member and sit with them hour or two. I commended this practice but I told him I didn't want him to do that. I enjoy being with people when I have a reason to be sociable. At this time I didn't want to feel obligated to entertain. After the service and luncheon for Elaine, a few of my family came to the house. I was in no mood for small talk and I anxiously waited for them to leave.

The day after Elaine passed, I wrote a letter to the facility and dropped it off. She was confined for eight months and two days. The letter read as follows:

23-Jan-2017

If I were to mention everyone who deserves my gratitude it would involve naming every employee of the Waters Edge facility. Rather than take a chance of missing someone, this letter is directed to each of you. The compassion and care by the staff never ceased to amaze me. How you can give of yourselves every day and keep a cool head is a gift that you should be proud to be blessed with.

I realize there were moments when I may have been too demanding. But, no one took offense and I am grateful for that. May I also say that Elaine was treated with respect and looked after as well as I could have done. Leaving her in the care of others was very difficult for me. However, it didn't take long for me to be comfortable with the arrangement. A special expression of my indebtedness goes to the girls who prepared Elaine for the mortuary. I will always remember how beautiful and peaceful she looked in her white turtle neck, her hair carefully brushed, her right arm across her chest and her left arm at her side. Elaine looked like the angel I'm sure she is. Thank you, thank you, thank you.

I also want to thank every one of you for making Elaine's last few months bearable. May God bless every one of you and reward you in ways you never thought possible. I will be forever in your debt.

Conrad

As I write this chapter, I mark the first anniversary of Elaine's incarceration in the nursing home. That day proved to be the most difficult of our lives. I often think that it may have been a mistake subjecting Elaine to spending the rest of her life in unfamiliar and uncertain circumstances. Everyone assures me that it was the proper thing to do. However, the doubt will always be with me. When I awoke this morning my first thoughts were of that dreadful day. I relived the details of that day and broke down.

My son John called this morning; he also remembered the date. He reminisced about how classy his mother was and how she always presented herself as if she were going to meet someone special. He remembers her in a most loving and caring way.

After Elaine's passing I took advantage of invitations from Heartland Hospice, grievance counseling services and a Westosha Senior Community Center class called, "Aging Mastery Program." I found it to be very beneficial to attend functions with others who have traveled the Alzheimer's road. Their experiences offered some guidance when I faced difficult issues.

For example, I would cry if I heard a song on the car radio that sparked a memory from the past. It happened spontaneously and it was a concern. At a grievance session at hospice the crying phenomenon was discussed and we were told it was common and that we were not losing our minds. By no means are my feelings or solutions to be regarded as prescriptive. Each of you will find the path that will be most constructive and suitable for you.

A few weeks after Elaine passed I was feeling ambitious, and decided to clean the basement. I came across the money that went missing while Elaine was still living in our home. A few picture frames were on a table and I curiously picked them up. Under the frames was the blue pouch with the money. I thought long ago that she had thrown the pouch in the trash and never expected to find it.

Soon after Elaine died I was invited to attend a presentation by a caregiver who spoke on the challenges facing a caregiver. After his presentation, the speaker asked for questions and comments. A woman in the audience commented that she didn't understand why some of her family members seemed disconnected and wouldn't get involved with the caregiving. I asked if I could address the comment and proceeded to share my experiences as a father of five sons; each of whom reacted very differently to their mother's stay at the nursing home.

Tom is very pragmatic and studied statistical analysis. When he and Bonnie would come to visit Elaine, Tom would say, "HI, Mom," sit down and engage in small talk. Sometimes he would kiss his mother on the cheek right before he left. Jim drove in several times from Nashville on Friday nights, spent most of Saturday with his mother and drive back to Nashville on Sunday morning.

John was a concern. Six weeks passed before he visited his mother at the facility for the first time. I didn't call him during that time because I knew he was struggling to come to terms with the situation. Craig's purpose was to make his mother laugh and he relished being able to brighten her day. Mark's goal was to comfort his mother with prayer. He would walk in and cheerfully and loudly say "Hello, Mother!" kiss and hug her, and kneel at her feet. Then he would hold her hand and recite the Our Father and Hail Mary. Even though each of the boys were born from the same Mother and Father, they displayed coping mechanisms that were vastly different. Everyone deals with new circumstances or a tragedy in a different way.

I was upset that several of our grandchildren didn't visit Elaine at the nursing home. I shared my disappointment with Mark and Jim and told them I would not welcome any of those grandchildren at the memorial service. They both convinced me of what I was trying to convey to the woman at the presentation was applicable to my situation. After a great deal of soul searching I realized they were correct and I dismissed any thought of not accepting my grandchildren's way of coping. I decided to respect their decisions to follow their own consciences.

After Elaine's burial, her grave site looked bare. I purchased a monument about two weeks after she passed and had an angel carved above her name. It was perfect. When asked if I wanted anything put on my side of the monument, I thought of an image that my sons might find appropriate.

Years ago, when my sons were young, I arrived home from work to find Elaine very upset; she had been having difficulty controlling the boys. I said, "I'll be right back," and left to retrieve a three-foot 2 x 4. I set it against the sink, looked at the boys and told Elaine; "the next time any of these guys give you a hard time, smack him with this board." I told the monument salesman the story in case my sons wanted a two by four engraved on my side of the monument. Elaine had often said that when she went to heaven, she wanted to be in charge of all the babies. Now that she's gone, I'm sure her wish has been granted. From the time Tom was born I marveled at how well she handled him. She was only 19 when our first son, Tom was born and she had a special way of calming him so he would feed well. No one ever taught Elaine about motherhood.

Tom, Jim, John and Craig are very close in age. At this time, Tom is 63, Jim is 62, John is 61, Craig is 60 and Mark is 56. As you can imagine, Elaine was very busy and had no one to turn to if we needed help. She was home raising the boys and it was her influence that helped form their good characters. Of course, they are all different, but they are each a product of their mother's love and care. I consider myself very fortunate and blessed for having Elaine as a life partner.

Adjusting to life without Elaine was tempered by the fact that she was in the nursing home for 8 months and 2 days before her death. I was accustomed to her absence in the house and at least that aspect wasn't an issue. Early on after her death, I awoke from an afternoon nap, and, still half-asleep, I thought I missed going to see Elaine. It was several moments before I realized she was gone. It was very upsetting and, for a moment, I thought I was losing my mind.

After Elaine passed, I left all her clothes and furniture at the facility. I was told everything was put to good use. I made occasional visits to the nursing home and brought along additional clothes or shoes for the residents. They were always grateful for anything I brought. I didn't realize how many of the women didn't have their own clothes or shoes. Many of those poor souls had few, if any visitors. Perhaps that's why some were so excited when my family visited. Particularly when they came with the young great-grandchildren, or when Mark brought his dog.

These days I often frequent the Westosha Senior Community Center and take advantage of the Senior Dining program there. The meals are well-balanced and it eliminates the chore of cooking for myself. I've met some interesting people there and have learned of other local places that offer very good-tasting, inexpensive meals. The fellows there ask if I might like to meet a woman to share lunch or enjoy a movie with. I thank them for their concern and tell them I really don't have any desire to have someone accompany me anywhere.

As they say, I may be gun-shy and don't want to be in a position of being a caregiver to anyone ever again. I never have or never will regret taking care of Elaine through her illness. She was my partner and that was the natural thing to do. My true love is gone and I don't believe I could ever devote my life to anyone else.

My time now has been dedicated to writing this story and in so doing I haven't had time to dwell on my loss. Now that I'm almost finished, I'm looking forward to remembering only the good things. I mentioned earlier that it has been difficult to rehash all those painful memories and I had no idea what an impact it would have on me.

At the time of this writing I had an unusual experience. I saw an article in the local newspaper about Alzheimer's and I thought about using parts of it in my story. Not being sure of infringing on copyrights, I went to the newspaper office to inquire about the possibility of quoting from the article without any repercussions. Two young girls were at the front reception desk which was quite large. I approached one of the girls and asked to see someone who may have answers to my questions. When she realized I was asking in reference to Alzheimer's, she said her name was Chelsea and she was a care-giver for a young disabled child.

After speaking to her for a short while it became apparent that we had something in common. She then asked me if I would let her hug me. The fact that we were both care-givers created an unspoken bond between us. She did come from behind the desk and gave me a hug. That hug was so sincere and innocent my eyes were beginning to tear. Receiving that pure affection from a total stranger was the best thing that happened to me since Elaine's death.

I couldn't help think how much happier everyone would be if we could substitute riots and protests with a little kindness. I find that love and kindness are much more palatable than discourse. Chelsea also made me realize how beautiful and compassionate people can be. No one from the newspaper was available to speak to me at that time and I never quoted the article.

Recently, Craig and I took a trip to see Jim and his daughter in Nashville. While there, the boys and I went to Huntsville to visit Joe and Mary. Joe and Mary knew the boys since they were three and four years old. Over the years we were more like family than friends and, as a consequence, a visit was always a treasured event. I get notions of selling the house and everyone advises me to wait at least a year before making such a major decision. It's probably best and I'll just have to be patient. The only thing I have definitely decided to do is to spontaneously pick a destination or someone to visit and go.

I sincerely hope our story helps to make your journey uncluttered and free of some of the foreseeable obstacles. Being a caregiver is a challenging responsibility and often requires help from others. For your own survival, I strongly suggest you don't hesitate to ask. I wasn't very smart, never even considered that I was a caregiver and seldom asked for assistance. It was only by chance that I became aware of the ADRC and the Alzheimer's Association. If only one person is inspired by our story I will consider it a success.

Don't let go of your Higher Power and always keep the Faith.

An Alzheimer's Request: (unknown author)
Do not ask me to remember; don't try to make me understand.
Let me rest and know you're with me, kiss my cheek and hold my hand.
I'm confused beyond your concept; I'm sad, sick and lost.
All I know is that I need you, to be with me at all cost.
Do not lose your patience with me, do not scold or curse or cry.
I can't help the way I'm acting. I can't be different though I try.
Just remember that I need you, and that the best of me is gone.
Please don't fail to stand beside me. Simply love me until my life is gone.

Dedication and Endurance

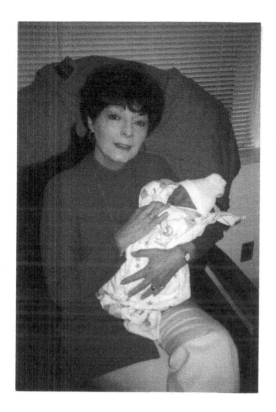

Elaine with babies. She always said she wanted to be in charge
of the babies when she went to heaven.

CHAPTER 13

"Reflections"

WHEN I FINISHED writing this story, and before they read my manuscript, I asked each of my sons to express their feelings in writing about their mother's last years with us. This entire chapter is dedicated to those feelings and they are placed in order of the eldest to the youngest son.

Tom Stevens, eldest. ("Stevens" due to a name change)

Mom's Alzheimer's was an experience that was a trial for her and the family. I live 5 minutes from mom and dad and therefore was able to provide support and help as needed. It was difficult to see mom's degradation and the strain that it placed on both mom and dad.

Mom had been deteriorating over the last few years, with the final 20 months being the most difficult. Dad worked tirelessly to care for mom at home, which put tremendous strain on him. He made a commitment to her that he would not put her into a home, which was a cause of internal conflict for dad.

The events leading up to mom going into a home were very rough on dad. Mom was difficult to handle and communicate with. Mom was constantly accusing dad of having someone else in his life, which was as far from the truth as someone could be.

Mom's sleep was impacted, with her being up all hours of the day and night. Dad had to ensure that mom could not open an exit door as the danger of her walking off was a grave concern. Not only from a safety perspective but also from a weather perspective. We live in Wisconsin and the winters can be very harsh. Mom's ability to communicate effectively was severely impacted, to the point that she was unable in many instances to find the words needed to convey thoughts. This was a very frustrating element of the disease. Not being able to know what the person was feeling, or needed.

I spent considerable time with them and also spoke with dad regularly so that he had someone he could share his frustrations and concerns with. We discussed mom's condition, the legal actions dad took so that he was positioned to provide mom with the care that she needed, and also to ensure that their estate was properly addressed, etc. As time progressed things continued to worsen, which brings us to the last 10 to 12 months of mom being with us.

It reached the point where dad was no longer able to care for mom at home. It was evident that mom needed to be in a care facility as she needed more care than dad could provide. This was a critical juncture, and the ability to move forward was in direct conflict with dad's commitment to never put mom into a home. This delayed getting mom into a care facility by at least 3 to 4 months. It became evident that dad could not do what was needed to find a care facility for mom, therefore I stepped in to address this issue.

I found facilities in the local area that were potential options for mom. Dad and I visited the facilities and selected one that was 15 minutes from their home. This minimized dad's travel time as he planned to and did visit mom every day. Working with the care facility dad was able to address the insurance issues, etc. and mom was admitted into the facility.

Family issues came up during this time as well after mom was admitted. I was the person responsible for sending e-mail updates to family members, brothers, etc. regarding mom's condition, how things were going etc. My communication was what I observed, no more, no less. This went on for quite some time until one family member took issue with what I communicated and went to dad to complain. Dad in turn took issue with me based on what the family member said. As of that incident I thought it best to no longer provide updates to the family. I didn't want to share my observations as they could become another issue and I didn't want to put any additional strain on dad.

During the time that mom was in the care facility the family issues continued to occur. This is how I approached the entire situation. I had to step up and be the logical, supportive, take care of issues person. This is how I cope with situations such as this. Emotions cannot rule as there were many things to take care of and I could not afford to be deterred in getting them done. I also continued to provide support during this entire situation, which again kept me focused on the logical perspective.

Others in the family approached this situation from an emotional perspective, which at times was in conflict with my approach. Family members could not understand how I could be the way I was. Their perspective was that I didn't care, that I was cold. What they didn't understand is that my love for mom was always there. It was that my approach to handling the situation was different from theirs, that's all. If there was anything learned which could be of use to others it would be this. Everyone handles situations in different ways. Just because they handle it differently than you do or you expect it to be done doesn't make them wrong. It means that they are different. They are doing what works best for them.

Another aspect of how I viewed this situation was that the person that we were dealing with for the last 8 to 12 months wasn't my mom. Mom was always a caring, loving, supportive person to everyone. Quick to invite you to sit down and have something to eat when you stopped by. Family meant everything to her. This is how I choose to remember her. I will say hi to her today from time to time as she meant a great deal to me. The person that Alzheimer's created was someone else. A person that wasn't happy, could not communicate, and was frustrated with the situation. My view helped keep me focused on the logical approach as well.

Mom's passing was a blessing. I was not sad. She is at peace. I like to think of her seeing her mom in heaven as her mom passed when my mom was 7. Mom cared for family very much, and I know that we all cared for her too.

Thanks, I hope that my perspective is useful and helps to bring some peace to you.

Tom

Jim

Hey Dad,

I'll do what I can to explain what I learned during the past few years in regards to the end of life process that we all go through in much different ways. I do not believe it is karma or a punishment or reward regarding how one dies, it is the luck of the draw. If it was earned, mom would have passed in her sleep. This is nature; it is the way it was meant to be. What gives me peace are the memories of the conversations I had with mom regarding death. I knew she was accepting of the inevitable.

Here is what I confirmed for myself during this process. Everyone will have a different approach to mom's condition. The range will be from one end to the other. The position one must take is one of understanding. If not, the result will be a drastic reduction in family members visiting. I found myself wishing mom would pass through the phase of being aware and reach a point of ignorant bliss. You then realize that is as much for yourself as for mom. It worked out the best it could give the circumstances. You were healthy enough to assist and mom had the care she needed. That was a blessing. I have no clue what you are dealing with. I do not want to know. If I can help, ask.

I was fortunate that I had a mother that held me accountable. Never one time had she made her love conditional. What a gift.

Jim

John

Here are a few words about my feelings for my mother. Her love not only for you, but for my brothers and I.

Her thirst for God's love that she shared with us and others she had come into contact with, she is a beautiful person, wife and mother. Her spirit will live with the angels. Her love for her family will always be there. Her love will grow stronger every day she is with God.

My mother believed in prayer. She always said to us, if you pray for it, you will receive it. Be true to your God and he will always watch over you and protect you. All you have to do is believe. It is truly amazing what the power of God can do in any situation. The presence of good brings order where we see none and transforms negative energy to positive thoughts and actions. With God all things are possible. Amazed by the spirit of God that heals and makes us new. Prayer came easy to me because I had followed what I was taught by my parents. My mother always taught us what was right and as the years progressed, prayer got a little easier. Thank you, mom. Love, John.

I feel mom is talking to us through these words and I do know deep down inside my heart she is with family having a wonderful celebration of life. She is smiling down on us. She is always watching over us. Her love lives on, and always will.

Love, John (your number three)

Craig

Thank God I was blessed with strong and loving parents. They taught us to be kind, have pride and be respectful to others. Parents that always showed me their commitment to each other and their sons. When I turned seven years old my mother got really sick. They told me she would not be around much longer. That *absolutely devastated me because I was going to lose the most pre-cious person in my life. Those were very hard years for my family. The six of us is what kept my Mom going. Her strength to live and to see her children grow was amazing. She never gave up nor did my father.*

When Mom was diagnosed with Alzheimer's I did not real-ize the severity of the disease. The first few years were not so bad because I only noticed her forgetting a word or two when she was putting together her sentences. The last two years for Mom were a lot more difficult. It was obvious Mom was very frustrated with her condition; it was hard for her to hold any conversation. To see her get so frustrated and start crying while she was trying to speak to me broke my heart. I realized early on it was best not to ask her any questions, instead I would do all the talking so she could just relax and listen. I found the best thing for Mom and me was laughter. So, I would come up with the goofiest things possible just to make her laugh, and that made it a good day for everyone.

When you start to hope that someone would gently pass away in their sleep tells you just how bad things have gotten. The last few months were horrible. At times, I didn't think she understood any-thing or know what was going on but at other times she would just cry. She was a gentle and loving person. She would hug everyone in the hall way at the nursing home. She brought warmth and love into a room. She definitely touched a lot of hearts before she passed.

I do not understand why such a wonderful, loving lady had to endure so much suffering. She went through Lupus, cancer and then Alzheimer's. My mother was a living Saint, no matter what she went through, her faith and positivity shined through. I also want to pay gratitude and respect to my father, he never wavered from adversity and always showed his love and commitment to his wife.

It was nice to hear from all my mother's nurses how they hoped their husbands would do for them what Dad did for Mom. It was so special to witness the respect my Father received from all the nursing home's employees. They saw a man completely devoted to his wife and it brought the whole family peace to know he was constantly by her side.

I also witnessed a whole other different side to Alzheimer's. My lady friend's father, George is a very soft-spoken man. I had no problem with George 99% of the time, but that 1% was a whole different side that was quite dangerous. One time we left him with a social worker to watch him so the two of us could go out. While pulling in the driveway we heard screaming coming from inside the house. George ended up yelling and hitting her. He was in such a violent and angry place at that moment. There were many times I would be alone with him and a violent side started to show. I learned the best way to deal was to leave the room and walk back in a few minutes later like nothing had happened.

Love you Mom,
Craig

Mark

My father requested that each son, "share your thoughts of your mother..."

Dedication and Endurance

July 7, 2017 Friday afternoon a bright and sunny day. The sky is scattered with snow white clouds that gracefully move in front of the incredible heavenly blue backdrop. And I keep thinking it is my mother's 83rd birthday restored and cared for by our Father. I can only imagine...the banquet table, the golden streets, like smooth glass, oh how amazing that must be.

I still miss my mother and I still would love to pick up the phone and talk, however God called her home and comfort is realized when my focus shifts from 'me' to God. There is great peace in surrendering to God when our season goes so very deep. A season filled with sadness, pain, despair and anguish but I have been blessed to have a mother that taught and exemplified faith in the Trinity. Her favorite saying, "Let go Let God" when life tosses you trials and tribulations we hand it over to God and Trust and He is with you always.

I am not sure how different things would be if I did not have this training from a woman of tremendous love, compassion and kindness for everyone she would meet. I am so very thankful that God allowed her beautiful influence to be a part of my entire life! I am also thankful that God's presence was evident during those difficult times. I recall walking down the hall to her room and the door was shut. Not typical for this environment. I slowly opened the door in the event she was being cared for and saw her lying on the floor after falling out of her wheelchair. Her shoe was near the window and her face was bleeding. She was shaking, moaning, sobbing and desperately trying to speak.

At this stage of her illness was unable to communicate verbally. I immediately got on the floor, cradled her head into my arms, rocked her so gently and told her "It's me, mother, Mark. God is with us, He loves us and you taught me that." I softly talked more words of encouragement into her for another 5 minutes as she slowly began to calm down. I then began saying the Our Father and Hail Mary for a few more minutes which allowed her to completely relax. What a blessing, I thought, when things returned to a sense of 'normalcy' that I still had my mother with me for 55 years. And to have a mother as amazing as she.

Through these past two years I have intentionally looked for the precious moments in the most difficult time of my life. Trusting God each day was invaluable and got us all through. There were many, many precious moments during my mother's transition.

My family and I have experienced my mother praying with people, hugging people, talking (in her language) to others and getting words out such as, "God loves you", "You're special" and her most consistent and favorite phrase shared with many, "I love you"! She talked about angels, family, both passed and alive and always had her eye on her husband. WOW what an incredible job my father did loving on her and being there. He went every day to her nursing home to brush her teeth, comb her hair and then sit with her, hold her hand and soak in the remaining days together here on earth. My father set the bar for commitment to spouse.

What amazes me most is how many precious moments occurred during my mother's illness. I could write a book on seeing God show up every time we visited. What a wonderful experience and to feel God's amazing peace and love during it all was the greatest blessing imaginable. I recall my father saying during the third month of my mother stay at Waters Edge, "How sad it would have been to miss experiencing all of these loving actions your mother is doing for all of these people." They happen consistently throughout her stay. Praise the Lord!

Below is a list of some of the Precious Moments:

Father and son relationships restored
Healing of hearts from past pains
New Respectful and loving communications realized
Genuine hugs from the heart
Honor
Growth
Tighter and intimate bond with God
Many shed tears
Humbling of the spirit
Maturity in faith
Truth
Scales removed

Happy Birthday Mother!!! I see you dancing with Jesus, surrounded by loved ones in the presence of our Lord, restored, joyful forever and ever, Amen.

Mark

Resources

Alzheimer's Association HOT LINE:	800-272-3900
Alzheimer's Association web site:	www.alz.org
Driver warning signs:	Healthinaging.org
Kenosha County ADRC:	262-605-6646
KAFASI (Kenosha Area Family and Aging Services, Inc.):	
	262-658-2263

Meals on Wheels

Senior Dining

Volunteer Transport

Daybreak (group respite care)

Family Support and much more

"Virtual Dementia Tour"

State and local services:	your state.gov
Transportation alternatives:	eldercare.gov
	800-677-1116
Westosha Senior Community Center:	262-891-3436

About the Author

Conrad Stroh was born and raised in Chicago, IL and currently lives in Kenosha, WI. He is a retired sheet metal worker by trade, a college instructor, former member of the United States Coast Guard Auxiliary, realtor, writer and inventor. He has been a loving husband, father grandfather, godfather and brother. His loyalty, integrity and generosity to his family have no bounds. He enjoys exercising,  eating out and keeping busy. He spends much of his time with family and buddies at the local Senior Center. In writing this book, Conrad has found solace, answers, guidance, peace and a voice. He hopes you find the same after reading this book. *Kelley Vari*